Brooklyn's Best

The Michael Behette Story

MARIANNA L. RANDAZZO

ISBN: 098948193X
ISBN 13: 9780989481939

This book is dedicated to my parents for the inspiration they provided every day of my life, and my grandchildren in the hope that I may inspire them.

Special thanks to my new friend, Madeleine Behette, and the Behette family for allowing me to share Michael's story with the world.

Thank you to all of Michael's friends, relatives, colleagues, and acquaintances whose memories have supplied an anthology of stories to fill this book and then some.

Thank you to my editor, Gerri Marino Friscia, who as always, makes everything I write look good. A special thank you to graphic and cover designer William Castello for his vision and expertise in designing this book.

Last, but not least, thank you to my husband, Gaspare, the love of my life, and my children Joseph and Jessica, Valerie and Kenny, and Gaspare and Melissa, who are always there to support me in all of my endeavors. I love you always.

"Many people will walk in and out of your life, but only true friends will leave footprints in your heart."

~ ELEANOR ROOSEVELT

.

Brooklyn's Best:
The Michael Behette Story

Forward

On September 11th, 2001, a cowardly attack was perpetrated against humanity in New York City, Washington D.C., and Shanksville, PA. But from the very worst of humanity, the very best of humanity would emerge. This book tells the story of Michael Behette, one of the many people who answered the call of duty that awful day.

As fires raged at the World Trade Center, and thousands of people evacuated to save their lives, many hundreds more ran into danger because it was their sworn duty. Firefighters, Paramedics, Emergency Medical Technicians, Police Officers and so many other first responders and members of law enforcement agencies responded to the World Trade Center to help. As the world watched, the greatest rescue operation the world has ever seen unfolded. Before the day was over, thousands of innocent people would lose their lives, including 343 members of the FDNY.

The New York City Fire Department is a large family of more than 15,000 men and women. When one member of a firehouse is in need the entire house steps up to help. On September 11th, the entire Department needed help. We were faced with a situation we had never before encountered and off-duty members from across the region responded to assist their fellow FDNY members. Michael Behette of Ladder Company 172 in Brooklyn was one of those Firefighters, but he had a far greater distance to travel than most.

Michael was in Florida on vacation that terrible morning. Like most people, he first saw the unimaginable situation unfolding on the news. But Michael was not like most people. Knowing he could not fly back to help the city and the Department he loved, Michael left immediately and drove all day and night until he was back home. And once he finally reached his home, he went to work. That's the kind of dedication to duty that makes New York City Firefighters so special.

In the weeks and months that followed, Michael stood side-by-side at the World Trade Center site with so many other FDNY members. Their mission was to bring home the 343 members killed that day and to give them the dignity and respect they had earned through selfless sacrifice. That difficult, but noble work would lead to the illness that would one day take his life.

Michael Behette lived a life very few get to lead. He was a son of Brooklyn who lived every child's dream of being a Firefighter. He lived that dream serving the greatest Fire Department in the greatest city in the world. He was an ordinary man who did extraordinary things and risked his life day after day to save others. His story is inspiring and it reminds us all of the impact one person can have on so many other lives.

Salvatore J. Cassano,
New York City Fire Commissioner, 2010-2014

Preface

People have always questioned what makes people like Michael Behette do what they do. What makes a fireman run towards danger when self-preservation tells us to do the opposite? What makes a police officer take the oath to uphold the law, to protect the rights of strangers, and if necessary, to lay down their own lives to protect another? These men and women perform heroic feats every day. They save lives, catch bad guys, and sometimes make the ultimate sacrifice; but mostly just work day to day, doing what they can to help, to serve, to keep order, and to protect. The September 11th rescue workers were hailed as heroes because of their swift actions under the extraordinary circumstances. What most people do not realize is that every day in a rescue worker's life has the potential to be an extraordinary circumstance, so it would be remiss to hail them as heroes for just one day.

Michael Behette served this city first as a police officer and then as a firefighter. Following in the footsteps of his parents, he joined the police force in 1981, working in NSU (Neighborhood Stabilization Units). When the opportunity to serve as a firefighter arose, Michael pursued that dream as well. He was a gentle and giving man long before the tragedy of September 11, 2001. Though the years that followed left him brokenhearted like so many others, it also left him even more dedicated to his fellow man. His passing at the age of 55 on September 17, 2012, eleven years after that tragic day, has left a void in the hearts of those who knew him well, loved him dearly, or were in some small way touched by his life. The latter consists of a multitude of people – those he saved from burning buildings, those he comforted and protected as a police officer, those he guided through career choices, and a young boy named Blake whose life he touched so profoundly during both of their last days on earth.

TAKING THE BLAME FOR ME
~ MARLENE DACKEN REMEMBERS

"Michael was a good guy. We met when my family moved to 83rd Street in Brooklyn around 1962 when I was five years old," remembers Marlene Dacken. "Michael was the smartest kid on the block. He memorized all the presidents in order and he knew all the models of the cars. Everyone knew he was just a clever kid. When his family moved from the six-family building to 85th Street, the friendships moved with them. Our families were very, very close. Christmas, Easter, New Years – we were always together, taking turns at each other's houses. Our parents were best of friends and we attended the same church – the Church of the Virgin Mary on 8th Avenue. We participated in the processions carrying candles on Palm Sunday and other religious holidays."

Not a day passed that Michael and his brother, Tony, didn't meet up with Marlene to hang out together after school. Kids knew how to entertain themselves in the street back then, relying on their imaginations and innate energy to invent games and keep themselves active and busy. Many a mother simply said, "You kids go outside and play," and the kids did the rest.

Bike riding, tree climbing, and skating were things kids could do with others or by themselves. Kids charted many miles just biking for the sheer joy of feeling the wind on their faces and the pedals under their feet. Tree climbing was a way to get a look at the world from a much higher vantage point and a way to play Manhunt. Skates were attached to shoes, and tightened with a skate key, which was usually worn on a string around the neck. Back then skating required only an alleyway, a sidewalk, or the street.

In those days, games like *Hide and Go Seek* and *Ring-a-lievio* ruled the streets of New York City. Although the rules were simple, the games required close teamwork and near-military strategy! In *Ring-a-lievio*, players separated into two teams, with one team going off to hide while the other team counted to a designated number before searching for them. When caught, the captor had to hold on to the player while shouting *Ring-a-lievio, 1-2-3, 1-2-3,* before bringing him or her to "base" where they stayed "imprisoned" until a still-free teammate tagged them and freed them. The game continued until all the members of the team were captured, the team gave up, or it got too dark to play. There was no parent involvement, except for providing a can for *Kick the Can*, a broomstick for *Stick Ball*, or bottle cap to fill with wax for a street game of *Skelzies*.

"Around dinnertime, Michael and I would compare notes about what our mothers were cooking. In those days, mothers cooked every night. Then we would decide whose house to eat over. Madeleine was like a second mother to me," Marlene remembers.

"Before we grew up and drifted our separate ways, Michael and I spent every day together and he was always protective of me. One day, Tony, Michael, and I were playing in his house. Often the boys played rough and this time something really big broke. It was probably something expensive and it made a loud crash. Michael's father came running into the room. Normally a very nice, quiet man, he was angry at his boys. I froze. Quite outraged, he asked who did the damage. Without hesitation, Michael said it was him, and took a beating from his dad, who was quite upset at the boys' shenanigans. He took his punishment without a word. I stood by, terrified and shocked. What his dad never found out was that it was not him– it was me! Michael hated when I told this story, but it is a true testament of the type of boy, and then man, that he became," recalls Marlene.

Like all good things, childhood fades and the moment comes when the door opens and lets the future in. But those were good times and good memories. Children played outside without any props or parents instructing us, and we had the times of our lives. Even though we ate a lot of candy, those activities helped keep us healthy, developed our bodies, improved hand-eye coordination, and gave us strength. Parents of the 1960s and 1970s certainly had the right idea about childhood!

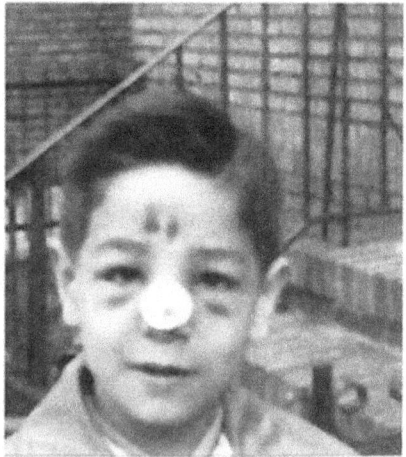

Childhood Days. (Top) Michael and his brother, Tony, with mom at Hicks Street and Atlantic Park in 1958(Bottom Left) Behette and Dacken families after mass (Bottom Right) Michael with a broken nose

LIFE IS A HIGHWAY
~ *KEVIN BOYCE REMEMBERS*

Mike's long list of friends begins with his childhood days in Bay Ridge, Brooklyn and in particular with Kevin Boyce, with whom he spent much of that time. Every Brooklyn kid knew where to get the best slice of pizza in his or her neighborhood. Many pizzerias served as landmarks and in the Bay Ridge pizzerias where Mike hung out, there was no dearth of good food and good times for the local kids. So it comes as no surprise that a great deal of childhood memories are intertwined with these eateries.

"Wow, where do I start?" asks Kevin of relating some childhood tales. "So many memories—might as well start at the beginning. I met Mike in 1971, when I was 13. We hung out at Rosemarie's Pizza on 85th and 5th Avenue with a 'cool' bunch of friends. We were all so young. We spent most of our time hanging out on Shore Road in Mike's basement, or at some of the local girls' houses. Eventually, we migrated all the way up the block to the Overpass. We would meet every night after dinner, just hang out, listen to music, and have a beer or two. I was attending Dyker Heights JHS at that time, where I met Pete Dontis, who introduced us to his friends from the schoolyard on 87th and Ridge. Mike and I would go hang out with them. What a great bunch of friends! At the same time, we met the crowd from *The Triangle* on 79th and 8th Avenue, who also became great friends. We spent our time at *The Sandbox* on Shore Road, in Bay Ridge, going to concerts at Riis Park, and at the Jacob Riis Beach— Bay 14."

Kevin Boyce continues, "We hung out at *Lyons Tavern* (aka the *Tender Trap*), *Pennington's*, and *The Hitching Post* among other places in Bay Ridge. It was just one good time after another. Everyone had their favorite hangouts and once you were in, the laws of society seemed to vanish.

When everyone got their first cars, it opened the doors to renting houses in the Hamptons, the Jersey Shore, and Hunter Mountain. I always shared a room with Mike. God, he snored! I used to put a pillow over his face.

The car rides up to Hunter Mountain were quite eventful. Mike hated cigarettes, and on one sub-zero degree trip, I lit a cig in the car. While driving, Mike started putting on his parker, with the fur-lined hood and gloves. I didn't give it much thought because, well, he was Mike. All of a sudden, all the windows opened and I heard him say, 'You violate my airspace; I violate your airspace.' I froze the rest of the way. In the summer, the same thing happened on way to the Hamptons. The temperature was in upper 90s. I lit a cig and all of a sudden the windows closed and the heat came on. I yelled, 'You're gonna kill us! They'll think it's a suicide pact!' Again I heard that familiar line, 'You violate my airspace; I violate yours!' After that, I refrained from smoking in his car.

A few fun-filled years went by when one rainy day, Mike rang my bell, shouting, 'Get up! You're coming with me!' He drove me down to Jay Street in Brooklyn and made me file for the police test. It was the last day of filing. That one day greatly changed my life, as I became a police officer six months later. Thanks Mike. Years came and went, and eventually Mike was the best man at my wedding, and then Godfather to my son Patrick. Throughout our 43 years of friendship, I think I spoke to Mike almost every day. There are just too many stories and memories to write. Thanks for everything, PAL! You changed my life. I think of you every day. May you rest in peace in heaven. I know you're looking down on me."

TICKET TO RIDE
~ GISELLE AWAD REMEMBERS

The 1970s were a decade famous for many legendary concert events. Bands like *Led Zeppelin* kicked off U.S. tours, sparking Rock concert fever, with many ardent fans attending multiple shows during a tour. Mike was a great fan of *The Who*, *The Rolling Stones*, and Frank Zappa, as well as the musicians that came to the local haunts in the neighborhood – musicians like Glen Miller and Jack Whitman, and the local band *Twisted Sister*. No matter if the Rock music was Hard, Soft, Punk, Heavy Metal, Blues, Glam, or Progressive; there were always plenty of great concerts being performed.

It was during these days that Michael began following his favorite groups, first at small venues and then traveling to countries around the world. It became his passion to fly anywhere in the world to attend a concert of his favorite musicians, like Paul McCartney and Billy Joel. His joy for music combined with the pleasure he derived in making others happy meant that he had no problem showing up at a concert and scalping a ticket if he knew a friend wanted to go. "I'll get you a ticket," he would promise. "It'll be good."

"Hey, what are you doing? Want to go to a concert?" Michael's cousin Giselle Awad recalls Michael beginning a conversation. "A few years ago, Michael was going to a *U-2* concert. When he told me about it, I got so excited because I also loved *U-2*. But disappointment must've also been in my voice. The next day, he called me back, 'Listen, I bought you and your sister tickets to go to the concert. I felt bad that I didn't

8

tell you about it before I bought my own tickets.' He was just as excited as we were, knowing that he was responsible for us going to the concert. After the concert, he called to make sure we had a good time. 'How were the tickets? How was the band? Did you have good seats? Could you see?' The show was amazing and so was he."

MEETING BUBBLES
~ *JOHN ALBANO REMEMBERS*

In 1974, John Albano worked in Bay Ridge at *Rosen's*, a famous toy store on 85th Street next to a simple soda fountain luncheonette with the name *Hinsch's* beaconing from a grandiose neon sign. *Hinsch's* was famous for their egg creams, waffles, Cherry Smash, and homemade candy and ice cream. At Christmastime *Rosen's* was known for their magnificent window displays and for their Santa, who stood outside handing out *Hinsch's* lollipops. Indeed, an afternoon trip to *Rosen's* and *Hinsch's* was a very special double treat!

For his 16th birthday, John Albano went to *Lyons Bar* with his friend Albert, who was already a regular there. (Keep in mind that the legal drinking age was 18 years old.) John recalls, "I got introduced to a bunch of guys and among them was a big guy with the strangest nickname– Bubbles.

"When we met at the bar, Mike kept saying, 'You look very familiar to me.' I shrugged, figuring he knew me from the store. A few days later, I'm in the back of the store, working in the stockroom. My boss called me out and told me there's a guy out front to see me. (Mike always looked older than he was.) I'm wondering who the heck wants to see me. When I came out, there stood Bubbles– whom I had only met once before. 'You get lunch, right? You gotta get lunch, right?' he said to me. 'Yeah, yeah, at 12:30,' I answered, wondering what he wanted.

"Standing beside me with his arm pointing out like a navigator at sea pointing to land, he started saying, 'Look, over there. I live right over there. You see it, right over there?' he repeated, pointing to his house. 'Why don't you come over? We'll have a really good steak sandwich for lunch, hang out, and have a Flying Saucer for dessert.'"

John went for lunch, and it was the beginning of a beautiful friendship.

"I remember it like it was yesterday. No one ever came over and asked me to be a friend like that. Lunch became a weekly thing. Then we would hang out at the Overpass with Jimmy Herro, on Shore Road with all the guys, or we hung out in his mother's basement. We were always in his Camaro on Shore Road. We were so tight, people joked that we were like boyfriend and girlfriend. We looked so much alike that girls mistook us for each other.

"One Saturday night, in the early 80s, Bubbles and I were at the bar in *Skinflints*. The place was crowded and loud, with people having a nice time," said John.

Skinflints has been around since 1975, serving great food for a long time, but it's the neighborhood clientele that gives the place its distinct flavor. Mike loved that feeling, and like many Bensonhurst and Bay Ridge residents, *Skinflints* was his go-to place for a juicy burgers served on English muffins, a beer, or some ribs.

Sitting at the bar surrounded by the original stained glass windows and tin ceilings, John Albano remembers Bubbles leaning over him because he was much taller, and saying, "You know, if we were to die tomorrow, next week, next month, or next year, some people would say, 'Yeah, I'm having a really good time tonight, but I'd be having an even better time if Albano and Behette were here!' He was so right and so profound for such a young guy.

"As he got older, he had a much larger lust for life, but he would say things like, 'I was having a good time before I was bored! Why am I so bored?' I would tell him to stop complaining, he had a good life.

"He looked around, and said, 'You're absolutely right.' He said, as only he could, 'I'm right, right?' Later on, he had such a zest for life.

"I have a very vivid, beautiful memory where we were all at Fort Hamilton, hanging out by the *Sandbox*. It was Jimmy and John Olsson,

Eileen, a few others, and me. There were three coolers full of beer and everyone was just having a party like we always did in the middle of the day. Those days everyone acted like they didn't have a care in the world.

"Bubbles pulled up in his Camaro, he gets out of the car eating an ice-cream cone! It may not seem strange now but if you think about it, everyone is trying so hard to achieve an unreachable state of happiness, and there was Bubbles with a big grin on his face. He was so happy just eating his ice-cream cone. Everyone started busting his chops about the ice-cream cone and he didn't care. He was the happiest guy there. It was the sweetest thing! How sweet was that? That this big guy, who could crush your head if he wanted to, could be so content eating his ice-cream cone!"

Evolution, Revolution
- *collectSPACE*

The chaotic social and political atmosphere of the late 1960s continued into the next decade. In 1971, as New York City was completing the South Tower of the World Trade Center making it the second tallest building in the world, President Richard Nixon was announcing his plan for a visit to China. His visit in February 1972 marked the first time a U.S. President visited the People's Republic of China since it was established in 1949. During this visit, President Nixon and Chinese Premier Zhou Enlai met to improve cultural relations between the two countries and establish trade policies.

Back at home however, America was suffering from a growing disillusionment of government. Michael Behette's mother, Madeleine, followed the news of the nation in English, a language she quickly mastered with the background she had received from the Salesian nuns during her childhood. If she feared the corruption in the new land, it was a topic she only shared with intimate family members.

The children of the 60s and 70s had the privilege of experiencing the golden age of space exploration. America's space missions *Mercury* and *Gemini* launched the first U.S. astronauts in space, while *Apollo 11* landed the first human on the moon on July 20, 1969. For those who were old enough to see that historic event, they remember that everyone on this planet stopped what they were doing to cram around a tiny, grainy television set to watch Neil Armstrong set man's first step on the moon, declaring his now famous quote, "That's one small step for a man, one giant leap for mankind."

Although more than half a billion people watched that historic moment, the majority of today's current population were not yet alive to experience Neil Armstrong and Buzz Aldrin's first steps on the dusty lunar soil. For those who did witness it, the memory is more indelible than ink. The 70s saw the Apollo program come to a close, but were dominated by the first orbiting space stations sent to explore the mysteries of the Solar System.

For Michael, these experiences kindled an interest he carried into adulthood, when an online community for space history enthusiasts, called *collectSPACE*, provided him the opportunity to interact with the heroes of his youth. Members of *collectSPACE* were deeply saddened by Michael's passing and shared these kind words along with a brief bio of his life:

A long-time member and frequent contributor to collectSPACE, Michael Behette died on Sept. 17, of lung cancer. He was 55. Michael was known to collect autographs from the astronauts he met and gift the astronauts he met with FDNY apparel and memorabilia.

Mike was a good customer. He sent us his picture of himself standing in front of the 9/11 devastation. He signed it and added "Never Forget." A few days later a package arrived. In it was small block of concrete. We framed them together in a gold leaf shadowbox. We won't forget. RIP, Mike.

Where Have You Gone, Joe DiMaggio?
~ Louis Riccardi remembers

There seems to be an incredible mystique surrounding the power of autographs. Michael was very passionate – and fairly successful – in collecting autographs and photos of his heroes, celebrities, politicians, and more. He even managed to put himself in a few of the photographs.

One old friend, Louie Riccardi, remembers Michael's fondness for attending autograph shows in Atlantic City. "An unforgettable moment in anyone's life would be meeting Muhammad Ali. There was actually a moment when Mike, Ali, and I had fists in each other's faces. Imagine that, sparring with the Champ!" Louie quips.

But the man that would leave the most indelible impression was Joe DiMaggio. "I was always late. I'm known as a procrastinator. The time for the showing was between 1 and 3 o'clock. I swear we got there by 2:30, but they were already closing up. Maybe the time was wrong, could be. Anyway, we went to go get a refund because those tickets cost a hundred bucks. The organizer took pity on us. I'm sure Mike talked his way out of us being late." Mike had that gift of smoothing things over, but what happened next was unprecedented.

"The organizer took us to the elevator," continues Louie. "We stood there in the elevator in that way that no one looks at each other, but just stares at the signs as the rotating floor meter went from Lobby to Six, and then Seven, where the doors opened. The only words spoken before entering were, 'I'll see what I could do.' Not far off the elevator in a hallway eerily silent, considering all the activity in the hotel, the organizer turns a quick left and before you know it, he's knocking on Joe DiMaggio's door! The door opens and from the secluded hall darkness of the hotel room, we could see Joe DiMaggio and a bunch of guys sitting around, watching a football game. He came over and talked to us as if he were expecting us all along!

It was somewhat surreal– like something out of the movie *Field of Dreams*. We talked about our favorite topic and common ground – Brooklyn. Mike and I made him laugh. It was a rare thing. We got to see Joe DiMaggio smile! We were like little kids, and the best part was that we shook the hand of the man who was married to Marilyn Monroe!"

(Top) Michael shaking hands with General Tommy Franks
(Middle) Mike and Louie Riccardi with boxer Muhammad Ali
(Bottom) Speaking with Governor Pataki at Ground Zero

A Changing World
~ Michael's Childhood

Many of the "radical" ideas of the 1960s gained wider acceptance in the new decade and were mainstreamed into American life and culture. Amid war, social rearrangement, and presidential impeachment proceedings, American culture flourished. Indeed, the events of the times became the inspiration for and were portrayed in much of the music.

Thousands of people filled Madison Square Garden in 1971 to attend the *Concert for Bangladesh*, the first benefit concert, in which George Harrison and Ravi Shankar teamed up to raise an unprecedented $10 million for UNICEF. Young people were becoming socially aware and were using the power of music to make a difference.

But music couldn't solve all of the troubles of the tumultuous 70s. National Guardsmen killed four students from Kent State University during a protest against the Vietnam War. The Watergate scandal caused President Nixon to resign to avoid almost certain impeachment.

As is true of every decade, there was a broad spectrum of events transpiring to balance the scales. Walt Disney World opened in Orlando, Florida. Louisiana unveiled the Superdome in New Orleans. Major League Baseball players went on strike—the first in sports history. And with the rapid growth of media, every event was followed via network news channels, radio stations, and daily newspapers throughout the United States. Families sat down to dinner with the 6 o'clock news spewing updates on Vietnam – America's first "television war."

This was the world Michael grew up in and, along with every child of that generation, the events and their repercussions profoundly affected him. But what happened in the Behette household was most traumatic of all for Michael. His father, George, who as a young man had traveled 6,000 miles to find a suitable wife and mother for his future children, became gravely ill. The once strong, robust police officer succumbed to illness, but not without creating indelible images of bravery and dedication in the minds of his two sons and daughter.

Michael's brother, Tony, remembers, "My dad worked a lot. He was definitely a 'cop's cop.' When my aunt, his sister, got married, I remember we were all at the wedding at the Church of the Virgin Mary on 8th Avenue in Brooklyn. The wedding ceremony was finished and the family and friends were standing outside the Church armed with rice and pennies, waiting for the new bride and groom to make their appearance to shower them with good luck wishes. Amidst all the excitement, a guy was running away from a cop on motorcycle. It didn't take long for my dad to see what was going on. In less than three seconds, I saw my dad tackle the guy to the ground and have his gun next to the perp's head! He was sooooo pissed because while tackling him, my father ripped his pants. That was in about 1970."

After George died, Madeleine was left alone in the world to raise her three children – Michael, Tony, and Marguerite. Madeleine recalls, "My youngest, my little girl, was only 6 years old, and Tony and Michael were teenagers. God had to carry me through that era—it was full of hippies and drugs, but the Lord carried me through it."

However, Madeleine was a tough lady on a mission to make her children the best they could be. Being a young widow from Syria, she kept to herself, demanding privacy from the neighbors and teaching her children to carry their pride in their hearts without being boastful or arrogant. Had they experienced any prejudice or discrimination, or had they been signaled out for being fatherless, it only strengthened their resolve. From her humble beginning, Madeleine had faith that

God would take her through life and turn these three children of hers into instruments of His peace and productive members of society.

Like many immigrants, Madeleine placed a high premium on education. She knew it was a necessity to survive. It was more important to her than the air she breathed, and it was with that determination that she achieved her goal of putting her children through private schools, universities, and medical colleges. "I gave my kids the best education: the love of a mother and father. I know Michael and the others appreciated all my sacrifices. I knew Michael especially took it to heart," she remembers.

In school, Michael had learned the story of Jackie Robinson, the young baseball player who broke the color barrier in Major League Baseball. What resonated with him were the sacrifices that his mother made for the family. "He would tell me the story of Jackie Robinson's mother, who worked so hard for her son. 'Ma,' he would say, 'you are like Jackie's mother—no one knows how hard you work.' I knew my Mikey appreciated everything I did. When Michael moved out, he told me continuously, 'At any time, any hour, you call,' and he meant it."

From Where We Came
– Young Madeleine's Story

In order to better understand the character of Michael Behette, you can look to his parents and grandparents and see the struggles and hardships they endured. His Syrian ancestry was one of pride, hard work, and tenacity. All of it helped shape Michael into the resilient, dependable friend he was to so many people.

Abraham Lincoln was once quoted about the influence his mother's prayers had on him. "They have always followed me. They have clung to me all my life." Such is the power of a mother's love.

Michael's mom, Madeleine, experienced her own mother's love only too shortly but its powerful penetration lasted a lifetime. Almost 70 years later, Madeleine could truly comprehend her mother's heartache and pain because, like Madeleine, she suffered the loss of children.

"It was back then that God carried me. I was left an orphan, motherless. A father could do only so much, and then nothing when left with six small children without a mother, my father was devastated," remembers Madeleine. When Madeleine's mother, Marguerite, was dying, she implored her daughter to carry on and do what she knew she could no longer do. "I depend on you," she besought the child who had been at her side always, especially during her darkest days of her babies' illnesses and deaths.

The family consisted of eight children, including two sets of twins. When the twin girls, Salwa and Samir, were three years old, they along with their one year-old brother, Elias, contracted measles. Sadly, the baby, Elias did not survive the disease.

When Marguerite became pregnant again, she prayed for a boy to devote to Saint Anthony. Because of Saint Anthony's fondness for children, it was common for mothers to place their babies under his protection and dress them in traditional Franciscan habits to thank and honor him. Marguerite was blessed with twin boys, Joseph and George. At their first birthday, she began dressing the twins in the brown habit every day, only removing it at night to prepare them for bed. She believed that following this custom would keep them safe. But her devotion to Saint Anthony was not enough to protect Baby Joseph, and he died at the age of 14 months. Baby George continued to wear the Franciscan habit until his second birthday on March 24, 1955.

The twins, George and Joseph, had both taken ill, but Joseph had continued to weaken until he was limp in his mother's arms. Together Madeleine and her mother walked the half-mile to the Sadate hospital, where they believed the doctors there could help. Young Madeleine, a child herself, carried baby Joseph when her mother's hernia slowed her down. As they entered the corridors of the Sadate hospital, Marguerite's concern went back to Joseph's twin left at home and the sores she saw developing on his small, tender lips. After consulting with the doctor and feeling comfortable enough to leave her baby boy in the hands of the respectable physician, mother and daughter hurried the half-mile back home to pick up baby George and carry him back to the hospital.

When she returned, holding George in her arms, Marguerite cried to a nurse who stood stoically by her station, "How is my son? How is my son?"

"He is dead." The cold- hearted nurse delivered the reply without a flinch, her words piercing the mother's heart like a steel knife. Her legs went limp, and she dropped to the floor. Her little son clung to her neck for safety as her screams and cries echoed the infirmary corridor halls.

On the wall was a poster with the directive "SILENCE, PLEASE." The nurse took her long bony finger, pointed to the poster as callously as she had delivered the devastating news and then brought the ugly finger to her lips.

Madeleine was sent home with little George. She would not allow them to touch her brother. Her mother stayed with the lifeless twin, refusing to leave her child's side. Back home, as the shocking news spread, the house filled with anguished relatives and friends. Madeleine remained home with the younger children as her father returned to the hospital with the formidable task of bringing his wife home. With their dead child swaddled warmly in blankets, their only thoughts were to keep him comfortable, bring him home, and mourn him properly. The taxicab ride (a luxury they could not afford) was filled with the heavy silence of parents determined not to disturb the "sleeping" baby.

With Joseph dead, Marguerite worried obsessively about George. The incessant worry turned into depression and her health began to fail.

Following World War 1, The League of Nations gave France a mandate to manage Syrian affairs. When Marguerite's health declined, she was brought to the French hospital where Dr. Charles operated on her hernia. Madeleine visited her mother daily, traveling via the city's only means of public transportation– an electric tramway. Although it broke her heart to see her so sick, she was grateful that her mother was there being cared for. Each day, she carried home her mother's handkerchiefs to hand-wash and return to her freshly laundered and ready to use the next day. This tiny act was a labor of love for Madeleine.

Although Marguerite returned home to her six surviving children, she was not recovering. She relied on Madeleine even more, always reminding her daughter, "Madeleine, I depend on you." No more was said, but so much was understood.

With her health steadily declining, Marguerite refused to go back to the French hospital. Instead, she chose to go to the Italian hospital and was examined by Dr. Conti. When the doctor saw signs of the recently performed operation, he inquired about where the surgery was performed and by whom. He knew something was terribly wrong, but he refused to touch her, instead suggested she go back to Dr. Charles for treatment.

Marguerite however, remained at home, weak and frail. Her abdomen was swollen and she was no longer able to bend or lift anything. She experienced bouts of nausea and vomiting. As the pain intensified, so did her darkness.

Nursing and caring for her mother at home became twelve-year-old Madeleine's daily routine, bringing bedpans and pitchers of water. She and her older sister Suad slept on a small sofa placed between the mother's bed and her father's bed.

"The day she died, I heard my father cry. I knew something was wrong. He sent me to get my uncle. 'Tell him your mother doesn't feel well,' were his words to me. I knew something was terribly wrong," remembers Madeleine. It was 3 a.m., a Wednesday morning, the 10th of November, 1954.

She hurried off, tears burning her eyes, when a loud voice bellowed through the night air. The man holding the traffic lights stopped her. "He yelled at me for running and crying. I was petrified, but I continued on my way to my uncle's door. When I arrived, I delivered the message to him. When they returned back to the house, she knew what little life was left in her mother was gone.

"The doctor said she had some sort of a staph infection. I believe my mother cried herself to death. My brother Joseph died on May 25, 1954, and less than six months later, on November 10, 1954, my mother was dead. Somehow, in all the confusion, I could see her broken heart, a heart that was shattered into a million pieces." It is that same heavy heart that Madeleine carries today for her beloved son, Michael.

After his wife's death, Madeleine's father found raising their six young children too difficult a task, so baby George was brought to the Salesian Sisters to be cared for. The Salesian family became Madeleine's surrogate family, filling the void in her heart. The nuns, however, were unable to keep the boy for long because the boarding school was for females only. Madeleine's father wanted his younger children to always remain together. He placed Samira, Salwa, Antoinette, and George in *The Two Sacred Hearts of Jesus and Mary Boarding School* in Lebanon. It was only the older girls, Suad and Madeleine, who remained in the house. Suad was the first sister to get married.

After Madeleine married and settled in America, she brought her father over. He then petitioned for her sister Antoinette, who had been put into a Catholic Boarding School. Two more sisters, 15 year-old twins Salwa and Samira, were novices in the convent at the time beginning the intensive spiritual preparation for taking their final vows. Their initiation into the religious life began after their mother's death when they were placed in a Catholic boarding school and were raised, educated, and nurtured by the nuns. But in 1962, before they took their final vows and committed their lives to Christ, Madeleine and her father offered them the opportunity to come to America. They took the offer and never looked back. The girls continued their education in the United States.

Madeleine and her husband brought George – the baby brother she had carried to and from the hospital on that awful day when his twin passed – to America as a student. Enriched with a valuable education and a sister's love, George studied and attended medical school. His studies lead him to a career in ophthalmology. Dr. George Kneisser was blessed with five children: George, age 29, a business owner; Marguerite, age 28, a lawyer; Joseph, age 26, a financier for L'Oréal; Elias, age 24, an Environmental Engineer; and Anthony, age 22, who owns a trucking business.

With the intercession of their mother Marguerite in heaven, Madeleine had fulfilled her promise to her dying mother.

(Top Left) Twins, Joseph and George, 1954,
(Top Right) Kneisser Siblings (circa 1962)
(Bottom) Najib and Marguerite Kneisser, (Michael's grandparents), 1939

Madeleine & George's Story

In 1956, almost two years after Marguerite's passing, Madeleine's sister Suad was attending mass when she caught the attention of George Behette, an American man visiting relatives in Damascus. He had come to Syria with his father in search of a girl to share his American home and life. George Behette was born in Brooklyn, New York in 1925. Despite his American upbringing, it was obvious that George preferred traditional relationships to the casual dating more prevalent in the United States. Perhaps the young man needed to find a woman who shared his cultural background, morals, and beliefs.

George inquired about the status of the tall, attractive girl with the mature demeanor. The priest informed him that he was too late. Sixteen year-old Suad had been married nine months earlier.

"Are there any more at home?" he inquired. Suad didn't know if her father was interested in considering a husband for her sister, but plans were made to visit the house. When George, his father, and some other men arrived, Madeleine answered the door and assumed they were friends of her father. It was not in her nature to ask questions, so she quietly went about serving them first lemonade and then demitasse coffee. After the visit, paying no mind to the small, diminutive school-girl, George inquired, "Where is the girl?" Shocked to find out that Madeleine was the girl, he showed no interest. She did not resemble the older, more mature looking sister, and he felt she was much too young to be a wife. He left and disappeared for a few weeks.

As his vacation time was nearing an end, he returned to the house to get to know Madeleine and reassess the situation. This time, he decided that Madeleine could indeed be a suitable match.

Meanwhile, this was not the first match that her father had arranged. With her aunt now living in the house, there was a lot of pressure to marry off the daughter. A young man had come to the house several times, but Madeleine was neither interested nor ready to consider marriage. Each time he arrived, she ran upstairs to a neighbor's house. During one incident when she tried to run, her father, who had a heavy hand and did not believe in sparing the rod, beat the girl in front of the suitor. The terrified boy came to her rescue and ended the suiting days after the incident.

The naïve young girl, however, was intrigued by George. Not understanding his foreign language, she depended on her aunt and his father to translate. She was told of his relatives in Syria, his life in America, his career as a patrolman, and his desire to find a wife from his father's homeland. Already quite mature despite her delicate demeanor, and well educated by the Salesian Sisters, Madeleine was the perfect candidate for such a proposal.

"Yes," was her answer. His magnanimity and graciousness won her over despite the communication challenges they faced. Her aunt conveyed the girl's willingness to consent to her father, who would have to give the final authorization or no arrangement would go forward. The young man was respected for his honesty, sincerity, and his financial success, and her father condoned the engagement. The couple was officially engaged on that very day. The wedding, officiated by eight priests and a bishop, took place on July 15, 1956 – one week short of Madeleine's 15th birthday. The church was full of the many Christian families from the village witnessing the nuptials. "He didn't speak my language and I didn't speak his, but somehow God had a plan," says Madeleine.

The wedding date also coincided with the end of his 31 days of vacation he had accumulated to spend precious time in the eternal city among the ancient buildings, lively markets, and bazaars where sellers peddled spices, sweets, rugs and all manner of tempting wares as they have done for centuries.

What began as a trip to visit his relatives in Damascus returned the tall, handsome George Behette to the United States as a married man, leaving his bride in the care of her father-in-law while he returned to his job as a patrolman in the 78 Precinct in Brooklyn, New York. He quickly began the paperwork to bring his bride to America. How little she knew about the almost 6,000 mile journey from Syria to New York and how it would change her life!

Madeleine waited in her homeland; sheltered by her father-in-law, and anxiously counted the days that would bring her to her new husband and to a land she had only learned about in books. On September 16, 1956, Madeleine made her first airplane voyage to America, escorted by her father-in-law. The girl had no travel experience so it was without knowledge or dismay that she embarked on her journey to America; her only fear was of the unknown.

Still unaware of how costly a trip such as hers would be, she sat without distraction observing those around her probably writing post-cards while smoking cigarettes, cigars, and pipes or enjoying a cocktail while awaiting a meal that was provided. Ironically, smoking was pro-hibited only on the ground for fear the lit cigarettes would ignite refu-eling fumes. Her new husband had gladly paid to bring his new wife to America, where the streets of Brooklyn, so foreign to her at first, would become her home for a lifetime.

Madeleine remembers, "Even though the marriage was arranged with-out us getting to know each other, it was a good union. My husband was very good to me. He was a good man. I lost him when I was only 29 years old. We only were able to share fifteen years of our lives to-gether. He was irreplaceable. I am ever so grateful he gave me my three children. He gave me my Michael– his oldest son, who was very much like him.

"When he died, my youngest child, my little girl Marguerite, was only six years old. Tony and Michael were teenagers and I was a young mother, a widow with three children, trying to do the best I could as both a mother and a father," said Madeleine.

*(Top) Wedding of Madeleine and George Behette, July 15, 1956,
officiated by eight priests and a bishop
(Bottom) Madeleine with her family before leaving for America*

Madeleine, George and baby Michael celebrating
her "Sweet 16", July 19, 1957

Bubbles
~ ROBERT AGOGLIA REMEMBERS

Although Michael certainly had a bubbly personality, that was not the root of his curious nickname. The truth is it came about one afternoon while a bunch of guys were hanging out in Robert Agoglia's basement, hooking up a four-channel stereo. Stereo components of the 1970's were big and heavy with metal fronts and lots of knobs, switches, wires, and lights. Those systems were designed to play the Rock music of that era and were arguably superior to today's equipment for listening to Led Zeppelin and Rolling Stones music.

According to Robert, "A few guys were hanging out– Mike, Vinny Charro, and me. Amid the blasting music, my baby brother, David, comes crawling into the basement. Mike loved kids and kids gravitated towards him. Michael swooped him up to play with him conversing with little David. Suddenly, out of David's mouth came the words 'Bub, Bub, Bub-bles, Bub-bles.' We all started cracking up! From that day the moniker stuck. He didn't exactly like the name, but it came about so innocently and it just stuck forever."

"Mike and I met at a keg party at the *Sandbox*. I had graduated from Xavier and had just left Brooklyn College for a year off, and that is when we met all the guys and girls that hung out at Fort Hamilton. Anyone who had a motorcycle, including me, had driven it to the party and then we moved the party to 1050-79th Street. I already knew some of the guys, like Sam Grillo and Jimmy Herro, from St. Ephrem's.

"We had a lot of good times during those days. Mike and I were like brothers– we had our love-hate relationship and spent the next thirty years hanging out, sometimes not speaking to each other for weeks, but still hanging out. For twenty years, we went up to our friend Greg's house in Hunter Mountain or we would hit the beaches on the Jersey shore. I knew Mike's favorite thing in the world to do was to put his chair at the edge of the water, put his feet in the sand, and read the newspaper. Of course, I couldn't just let him relax and have his fun. I teased him that he was a woman trapped in a man's body. Of course, I was taking my chances saying that because Mike could've easily snapped me in two, because in truth he was more like a heavy-duty wrestler trapped in a human body.

"I'm pretty sure Mike never told many people at the firehouse his nickname was Bubbles, but to those who knew him when, the name will always stick, with love," Robert remarked.

1968
~ A Flash Point Year

In 1968, Madeleine, a patrolman's wife with several years of English under her belt, was sought out by her country for her expertise in the Arabic language. With her oldest son an 11 year-old, a second son not much younger, and a baby girl at home, Madeleine was called upon for her unofficial skills as an interpreter. Her husband, George Behette, was a patrolman in a Brooklyn precinct, capable in English and Arabic (his father's native tongue) but not as proficient as his wife, who had almost mastered four languages in her short time in America. The NYPD needed assistance, and young Madeleine was someone that could help them on these matters. Madeleine had been acclimating to American life when the request came along. She was needed to interpret documents from Arabic to English in an effort to ensure the safety of the President of the United States. Her only concern was taking away time from her three precious children.

The police department and the Secret Service did not see that as an impediment; they made acceptable working arrangements for her. While her sons were being boys, playing ball, riding bikes or fishing on the 69th St. Pier, the young mother diligently translated documents to assist her newfound country. It was not in a government-secured office that these translations took place – it was at her kitchen table and the classified documents were removed from an overstuffed valise that the NYPD had uncovered. Daily, the newspapers reported that "translators were working diligently to uncover classified information." Every day, between breakfast, lunch, dinner, and into the night, the diminutive foreign-born girl, educated by the Salesian nuns, did for her country what trained professionals were unable to accomplish.

During the period while Madeleine translated, her husband became caretaker of the children. Their roles were switched, and the NYPD compensated them. Unknowingly, Madeleine aided in the national security of the country, a country her children had the right to claim as their own. When her mission was over, it was back to being a housewife and mother.

It was then that Madeleine realized the education endowed upon her by the Salesian nuns was invaluable and an asset that would carry her for the rest of her life. Her language skills became more acute with each paper she translated and her knowledge of police matters multiplied, later leading her to make life choices she could never have imagined when she was a little girl.

That year, one of the most tumultuous, disruptive, and frantic years in American history, was a flash point for the many transformations for which the 1960s is known overall. The events signaled the powerful cultural, economic, and social changes that still reverberate today. While Michael probably watched with amazement, NASA launched Apollo 8 on December 21st, and on Christmas Eve, Americans watched a live broadcast as it became the first spacecraft to orbit the moon and return to Earth. Little did Madeleine know how her own home and life would change forever.

(Top) The wedding of Mike's Parents, 1956
(Middle) Family Photos
(Bottom Left) Mike, Tony and mom at Coney Island
(Bottom Right) Marguerite's first birthday party, 1965

*(Top) Michael and Tony dressed in sailor suits with Dad
and Granddad. Hicks Street, Brooklyn, 1959
(Bottom) Marguerite, Michael, Tony and relative in Lebanon, 1969*

Patrolman vs. Policewoman
~ *Madeleine remembers*

"In late 1968, two policewomen, Lucy Accera and Vittoria Renzullo, came to our house and cooked an Indian food dinner for us. They were friends with my husband, George. We had known each other for several years and they knew about the work that I had done translating for the police department.

"After dinner, Lucy pulled me aside. 'Madeleine, I've been thinking,' she said. 'The test for policewomen is coming up and I think you should take it.'

"I was shocked to hear her say that. It wasn't something that I had never considered and I knew my husband would never consider it for his wife.

"She reminded me that I had done translating work for the police department for free in the past. 'Why not get paid for it?' she asked me. I said that it was a good idea but I didn't follow up on it. My husband did not go for the idea – he told me and Lucy, 'I didn't go 6,000 miles to get a wife to become a policewoman.' The discussion was closed for a while.

"That summer, I took Michael and Tony to Syria to visit my family. It was a bit of a difficult trip for us. Michael hated the toilets and refused to use them. I had to leave my boys for a few days to visit my husband's uncle in Lebanon. I left my boys at the convent with my dear friends, the Salesian nuns and the Mother Superior, confident that they were in good hands. I made the trip alone to speak to my husband's uncle who was a powerful and wealthy man. I needed him to help me find employment for my father, who had been out of work. While I was over 80 miles away, I found a telephone to call the nuns to find out how my boys were. They told me Michael had fallen ill and was in the hospital. I immediately made the 80-mile journey back to find out that he had caught some bug, and Mother Superior had stayed with him night and day in the hospital. He recovered and we went home," remembers Madeleine.

"While I was away, I gave much thought to what my friend Lucy had suggested. Back in my Brooklyn kitchen, I decided to give her a call and find out more about the test. It was 1969."

In those days, they were policewomen and patrolmen. They only took a handful of policewomen, and they never went on patrol at that time. Their jobs were female-only duties: they were given desk and clerical work, sent to women's jail wards, or posted to juvenile investigations units. On top of that, they faced old-school stereotypes and biases. So many men and women couldn't imagine why a woman would even want such a job!

They were required to wear impractical skirts, caps and they were required to keep their guns and handcuffs in a purse, which was very impractical and expensive, according to Madeleine.

"It was definitely a male-dominated profession, but I decided to give it a crack anyway," says Madeleine. "After all I had experience with the police department, and I was married to a patrolman. That day, I called Lucy and expressed my interest. She went into a panic. 'Madeleine today is the deadline for you to register to take the test!'

"What should I do?" I asked. "I followed her directions. I had to get to 49 Thomas Street, in New York by 4:00p.m.. Now, *I* was in a panic. I went to the subway and asked how to get there. I didn't know where the hell I was going. I took the train to City Hall and walked to the place. I made it and registered to take the test. The next step was to study, to prepare for the test. I found out they had a prep course at Gallante Institute. I never heard of that either, but I found my way there, only to find out it was the last day of the course. Everything was going against me. I also realized that thousands were taking the test, and that only 40 or 50 would be chosen. They also told me it could be five years before I would hear from them.

"I just kept going. The test was coming up, so I decided to do the best I could. On top of everything else, I had to get a G.E.D. because I had gone to school in Syria. On the day of the Policewoman's test, for the first time in my life, I was exposed to multiple-choice answers. I couldn't believe it! The answers were right there. I took the test and scored very high, especially for someone who had not prepared. Fortunately, my education prepared me for that test and I passed.

In those days, they gave you the test results in *The Chief*, a civil service newspaper. "I scored an 88," remembers Madeleine. "Lucy told me that if I were a man, they would take me *like that*, but because I was a woman, I had to have 100 or better, even 110. Sometimes you got extra points for working with the city. She told me not to get my hopes up too high.

"Okay, what could I do? I forgot about it for a while. Two years passed, and in 1971 my husband George passed away. One day at the end of the year, I come home from the store and I see note on my table – one of the kids took a message. An Officer Rodriquez had called. I searched my brain thinking which one of my husband's friends it may have been. I return the call. I explained that I was Patrolman Behette's wife. They asked if anyone in the house had taken the Police Exam. I was dumbfounded. It was for me. Almost three years had passed!

"When I graduated from the Police Academy, I wore a skirt and had to buy an expensive leather pocketbook to keep my gun in. I was put in a Manhattan Traffic Area. Things had changed. For one thing, we were all called Police Officers – no more Policewoman or Patrolman. They assigned me to Manhattan Traffic on the West Side Highway until it collapsed. The highway had decayed so badly that it had to be permanently closed 1973," said Madeleine.

"After traffic patrol, I was put in the 17th Precinct at 167 East 51st Street. It was in Midtown North, and a great place to be stationed. I was near the United Nations, the U.S. Mission to the United States. I met so many dignitaries, public figures, and King Hussein got to know me by name.

"By 1975, when my boys were teenagers and Marguerite was still a little girl, I got laid off from the Police Department. The city was close to bankruptcy.. It wasn't just us, there were massive layoffs, and piles of garbage were in the street because of Sanitation Department cutbacks. There was a dangerous decrease in police patrols due to layoffs," recalls Madeleine.

Not even the President wanted to help New York City. The Federal government, through President Gerald Ford, promised that they would not bail the city out of the mess it had gotten itself in. That prompted the New York City's *Daily News* to print the headline: "Ford to City: Drop Dead."

"I was out of work. Some cops took other city jobs. My friends Loretta and Fran became bus drivers. I didn't want to drive a bus. A year later, I got called back. I was one of the first ones called because I didn't have a job. I returned to Midtown North. It still wasn't easy being a woman in a man's job. Many of the girls were harassed. They tried to make some peoples' lives hell by giving them terrible posts and awful hours. I was still very happy with the job.

"Years later when my son Michael was a police officer and so was one of his best friends, Kevin Boyce, I had been working in Brooklyn's Central Booking. Although I loved working in Midtown North, it was too far and I preferred working in Brooklyn. I was transferred to Central Booking.

"I loved that job too, and I had fun giving the Highway Patrol Cops a hard time. Whenever they showed up, I made them sit and wait and wait and wait. I figured if they were off the highway, they couldn't give tickets. They would've given their own mothers tickets. It was an awful detail. If they didn't meet their quota, they were taken off the detail.

"One day, I get a phone call from an officer at the Tombs in Manhattan. It seemed Manhattan's Central Booking didn't want his prisoner.

'What's your name, Officer?' I asked.

'Officer Boyce,' he replied.

'What's your full name? Shield number? Registry number?' I demanded. Growing inpatient he answered accordingly. I could sense his annoyance.

'Are you sure that is your name, Kevin Boyce?' I asked indignantly.

'Yes, I'm sure,' he answered with an attitude.

'Are you sure your name is not Misery #2?' I asked, referring to the pet name I had given him, respectively calling my son Michael Misery #1. Silence followed.

'Mrs. Behette? Is that you?' he asked.

'Sure it is,' I laughed. 'Bring your prisoner over. I'll book him.'

"Kevin couldn't believe what I had put him through," laughed Madeleine.

"Over the years things changed in the Police Department. No more shoulder bags for our revolvers. Women were allowed to take promotional exams. The exams became gender-neutral and in 1976, my friend Vittoria, who came to my house to cook an Indian dinner for us, was now Captain Vittoria Renzullo and had become the first female to be assigned as a Commanding Officer of a Precinct, at the 1st Precinct in Manhattan!" proudly declared Madeleine.

(Top) George Behette, Navy, 1941, Patrolman George Behette, 1951
(Bottom) Appointed Policewoman Madeleine
Behette, 1973, Police Officers, 1982

Teenage Wasteland
~ Jimmy Olsson Remembers

"Experience is simply the name we give our mistakes."

~ Oscar Wilde

"Mike and I first met at Fort Hamilton High School on the bleachers listening to music," recalls Jimmy. "Most of the people there were cutting out of school or had just stopped going to school. Not us, of course.

"It was the early 1970s and a lot of stuff was going on. A lot of time has passed, but I do remember Mike was a nice guy and it was the beginning of a great friendship that lasted a lifetime.

"As the years went on, we became even better friends. There were a few of us that remained friends until this day: Jimmy Herro, Kevin Boyce, Sam Grillo, Gaspare Randazzo, Kevin Boyce, and Louie Riccardi, just to name a few. Everyone would meet by Fort Hamilton High School or the park across the street. Some of the guys didn't even go there; Sam and Louie went to Xaverian, Gaspare went to Lafayette, but Mike and I were Fort Hamilton kids. After the days at the park, we began hanging out at the local pubs, like *Nook and Crannies, Beards, 2-Morrows, Skinflints, Tun's Tavern, Hitching Post, Horsefeathers* and *Hammerheads*. The list goes on and on. Bay Ridge had no shortage of bars, and although there was a drinking age, nobody really enforced it back then. Not that we abused it or anything like that!

45

"The years went on and the crowds grew bigger. Mike and Kevin would show up at the *Triangle* and hang out with us. We used to hang out every day. Then everyone started meeting other guys and discovering new bars. Mike hung out with the guys from *Lyons* 87th and 3rd—we played darts with them.

"Mike was one of the only guys who had access to a car – it was his mom's. This gave us access to the great big world outside of Bay Ridge, which leads us to the story that I call *The Night of 1,001 U-Turns*," laughed Jimmy.

"Sam, Louie, Mike, and I all went up to Russell's parents' house in Warwick, New York. We were all between the ages of 17 and 19. After hanging out all day and having had a few drinks, we decided to go for a ride in the woods. We assumed Russell knew where he was going, which was clearly a poor assumption. Russell decided to take his .22 rifle with him.

"Of course this story could have some inaccuracies in it as I may have had some memory lapses over the years, maybe even back then," admits Jimmy.

"We had been partying for hours, and Mike was the only one able to drive and it was his mother's car. There were so many of us squashed into the car, I barely remember the seating arrangement, but I do remember Russell sitting in the back with the rifle perched upright between his legs. Now, keep in mind we were in the country, so it wasn't unusual for people to drive around with rifles and there was never any mal-intention. Also keep in mind that .22's are used by Boy Scouts to get their shooting merit badge and they are sold at Walmart!

"It was after sunset on a fall night and the fog was as thick as pea soup – the kind of fog you find in England. It definitely created a visibility hazard. To top it off, we were lost! Driving in that fog was like driving with blindfolds on. We could only see as far as the headlights allowed visibility, and that's not taking into account our own limited senses.

"Meanwhile, the fog rolled in even thicker. We had no navigator except Russell, who was useless and in his own fog. We drove for 20-30 minutes in one direction, but we couldn't find a corner or a street sign or any sign of life. The long and winding roads led to nowhere, so about every 20 minutes, Mike would make a U-turn. He seemed to be the only one making a conscious decision to get us out of the clouds – after all, he was the driver. With the music blasting as loud as the car speakers would allow, and all of us singing to our own tune, it was hard to distinguish any sounds. We drove around aimlessly, making U-turn after U-turn.

"Finally we saw headlights in the fog coming towards us. Mike opened the window as the car lined up with us in the opposite direction. It was the worst-case scenario – it was a cop! Things could've gone any worse. 'You boys aren't drinking, are you?' the cop asks, with a flashlight shining on each of our faces, as we may have been kicking beer cans under the seats.

"Of course, Mike talked for us because most of us couldn't even speak and the idea that a cop would stop to help us left some of us cracking up. Mike managed to get the cop to give us directions back to Russell's house, but I think he was really trying to just ditch the guy before he got too curious.

"The directions didn't help; we continued to drive and crack up. Between the music and the laughing, the noise in the car was loud enough to cover up an explosion (which we later found out it did!). We were pretty much null and void.

"Somehow, we made it back to the house. The next morning or probably afternoon, everyone rolled out of bed, and while outside someone noticed that in the car, about an inch away from where my head touched the roof, was a hole burned into the roof.

"Not sure who had the nerve to say it, but someone asked Mike how he got that hole in the roof of his mother's car. Everyone started examining the hole. A trajectory analysis of the hole pointed to the .22 that was perched between Russell's legs.

"Needless to say, it wasn't a pretty sight. Mike didn't hold back, and idiots that we were, we started cracking up and trying to come up with stories that he could use! After all, his mom was a cop. 'Tell her someone opened an umbrella in the car' was the excuse of choice. 'Tell her it was like Mary Poppins!' Each suggestion was answered with his usual 'You suck!' remark. 'You think my mother's going to believe that? She's a cop, you jackass!' he snapped. Mike was pissed off. He knew his mother wasn't going to buy any of that nonsense.

"Not sure what happened when he got home, but about thirty years later we did admit to Mrs. Behette what happened. I'm sure she knew all along! There wasn't much that got by that woman," remarked Jimmy.

"A few years later, Mike was a fireman and working the night shift. He was looking forward to hanging out with all the guys at Mikey 'Hot Dogs' house in Hunter Mountain. Problem was that we had started the party without him, while he was still working his job. After his shift, he drove three hours to hang out with us, but by then we were done! He walks in the house and finds everyone lay out askew. It looked like a crime scene; we probably all looked dead," remembers Jimmy.

"He walked around and was pissed off that that no one was alert enough to hang out with him. I guess he was not impressed with what he saw. 'What the ****? This sucks!' he announced to anyone who opened an eye to see him there. He got back in the car, disgusted. He had worked all day and wanted to have fun. Pissed off, he drove all the way home.

I Can See Clearly Now
~ 1976

The year of our nation's bicentennial, 1976, was a triumphant one. On the eve of July 4th, a program of patriotic songs was performed in Central Park. The next morning, more than 200 tall ships, under 31 flags from around the world, chugged up the Hudson from the Statue of Liberty. Hundreds of thousands of New Yorkers dotted the shoreline in places like Shore Road in Brooklyn, roaring on cue when the 21-gun salutes began at noon. The police estimated that there were six million people who viewed Operation Sail from the New York shores, and there were also large numbers who viewed it from New Jersey.

That was the year Michael decided to attend the New York City College of Technology in Brooklyn. He studied to become an ophthalmic dispenser, better known as an optician. Not many of his friends were aware of this path he had chosen.

By the next year however, the climate in the city had changed drastically. During the summer of '77, a serial killer stalked young couples with a .44-caliber pistol. A power failure plunged the city into darkness and ignited widespread looting. It was the summer when Billy Martin and Reggie Jackson nearly came to blows.

Michael began working in an eyeglass store on Lexington Avenue in Manhattan, fitting people for eyeglasses and contact lenses. He hated it and was probably bored to death! Working at the counter, he had to deal with all types of characters. One morning, a prominent Manhattan politician, whom Michael described as a "pompous ass," walked in. The man had dreams of becoming mayor and beyond. This is how Michael told the story to his friend John Albano:

"He comes in all pissed off and has to come to my counter. Without even looking at me or saying hello, he throws down a receipt and says 'Are these ready yet?' with an attitude.

"I take the receipt and go to look for it, but they are not finished yet. I then go back and deliver the news.

He starts yelling! 'What the hell is wrong with you people? They were supposed to be ready a week ago! I never saw such incompetence in my life!'

"Really?" Mike replied, "And what do you think of the people running the city?" With that, Mike walked away and let the store manager deal with it.

It was a very short-lived career. In the end, he confessed to his mom, "I just couldn't stand putting glasses on people's noses all day and waiting for them to make decisions!"

P.S. The politician never made it to the mayor's office.

Right Place – Wrong Time
~ Gaspare Randazzo remembers

"In 1977, becoming cops was not in the works yet," recalls Gaspare Randazzo. "We went to see Led Zeppelin and parked the car on 34th Street, illegally, and headed towards Madison Square Garden. The show was explosive, literally. It was an amazing show. People remember John Bonham's drum solo being incredibly long and the kettledrums being ear-busting.

"When we got back to 34th Street, we couldn't believe someone had stolen the car! We found a phone booth quickly, because in 1977 they were everywhere in public places, airports, train stations, convenience stores, malls, casinos, and on street corners. We called 911 to report the car stolen. After they laughed at us, we were told that the car wasn't stolen, it was towed. What a surprise, parked right there in a tow-away zone, the car actually got towed! We got on the subway paid the thirty-cent fare to go to Brooklyn to get money and then got back on the subway to Manhattan; the conditions were so deplorable, it was amazing that the trains even ran. Riding the dark, stinking trains completely covered by graffiti, I couldn't get to where the car was soon enough. Mike and I got to the tow pound and paid the towing fees. Luckily, there were no outstanding tickets. That was an expensive concert and lesson," remembers Gaspare.

Born to Run
~ Jimmy Herro remembers

Mike was inpatient and he drove as fast as his Camaro could take him. The sound of that Camaro made an incredible sound until it stopped in front of Jimmy Herro's house and he heard the famous howling cry of *Herrrr-oooo, Herrrr-oooo*. It didn't matter if the neighbors looked out the windows or kids on the sidewalk stopped playing to look, Mike had arrived and Jimmy had to be ready to go.

The stop was only long enough for Jimmy to hop into the car before the tires started to spin in place and within 15 seconds the car accelerated to what felt like 60 miles per hour. If it had not been for the Stop signs, within a minute he would've been at 120 miles per hour.

Well, that's how it all seemed back then in the summers of 1977 and 1978.

There were no cell phones to call your friends as you approached their houses. You made one phone call from your house phone, if any, or you just made a plan the night before. The thing about Mike was that he never wanted to waste any time. If you weren't ready, he just as well left you behind, but being a good guy, he'd always come back to get you.

"Mike would honk the horn and scream my name in his low, baritone voice. I knew enough to be ready and off we went to Riis Park Beach. To get there, we had to cross two bridges and go through Broad Channel. Once there, the day was ours.

"Mike had such a great spirit, he enjoyed life. Years after our teenage years, I lived in Fort Lauderdale, which gave Mike a place to visit. He visited me often. On one occasion, he wanted to go to Disney World for a couple of days. There was not a ride that Mike missed on that trip, even the kiddy ones!

"Besides hanging out at the beach as often as possible, back in the mid 70's we did a lot of camping. We would hike up to Spruce Pond Boy Scout Camp only to get kicked out after hours of lugging coolers and beer up the mountain. Michael's famous words were, 'Every time I go camping with you, it turns Into a Survival Mission!' Things did tend to get out of control," admits Jimmy.

"In the later 70s, we would go car camping. Some of those trips were up by near Warwick by Russell's house. There was a Boy Scout camp there too. We went up there twice in one month – a week apart during the month of April. Both weekends it rained very hard. Michael was known for his love of pizza and ice cream. (We came from Brooklyn, home of Pizza Wagon on 86th Street and 5th Avenue and Baskin Robbins.) Well, on both of these weekends, Michael woke up on Sunday morning and wanted ice cream, but we weren't in Brooklyn anymore! The only way to get these luxuries was to get in his car and drive out of the camp and down into the village of Warwick, a town that boasts a beautiful rural setting just a stone's throw from New York City, untouched by excessive development. They weren't kidding. The private campsite was on state land, and was comprised of all dirt roads. We probably shouldn't have been there and Mother Nature made sure we were duly punished. Michael's car ended up getting stuck in the mud on both occasions, trying to get to an ice cream shop. I guess he didn't think he could be that unlucky twice. Even with all of our maneuvering skills and surveying the lay of the land to get out of the mud, it didn't work. He was pretty far gone in the mud. We had to call a tow truck and that meant going back to Russell's house to use the phone. Each time we had to get out of the same spot, you can imagine how happy Michael was waiting for that truck. He never got to eat his ice-cream!

"We did grow up and do some adults things, sometimes!" admits Jimmy.

"Year later, Kevin Boyce, Mike, and I went to a very expensive popular restaurant in Fort Lauderdale. We were all pretty hungry and looking forward to a good meal. Mike orders himself a filet mignon, probably the most expensive item on the menu. It never mattered to him. When his meal arrived – almost special delivery – it came on a silver-plated serving dish that probably was about 12 inches in diameter with a lid on it about six inches tall. Mike's eyes lit up. Everyone's eyes lit up! We looked at our paltry plates. Mike peaked under his plate while everyone else was being served. The expression on his face turned from ecstasy to agony. 'What is this?' he said in disgust. 'Did you see this?' He lifted the dome off of the saucer and there sitting on a shiny silver plate was a piece of filet mignon the size of a hockey puck! His face was priceless! Everyone at the table cracked up! Actually, it was much smaller than a hockey puck, maybe one-quarter of the size," remembers Jimmy Herro with a smile.

Yo- Yolanda!
~ *Yolanda Garcia remembers*

"I have had a crush on Michael since my high school days. He was older than me; I was 16, and he was 19. He was always, nice, polite and sociable, but that's where it ended. We were friends," reminisces Yolanda.

"Our lives moved on, I got married, had my daughter, and moved out of state. I was gone from Brooklyn for many years.

"After my divorce, when I returned to New York with my daughter to be closer to my family, I reconnected with my high school friends.

"Michael and I ran into each other at the Octoberfest in Bayridge. At this point, we were both in our mid 30s – no more age difference. He asked me if I wanted to go to *The Who* concert. Of course I wanted to go! I assumed we were going as friends.

"We went to the concert had a wonderful time and that night, the fantasy that I had so many years ago became a reality. We became boyfriend and girlfriend.

"Mike and I started spending most of our time together. Whenever my daughter was with my parents, at a friend's house, with her father's family, and when she went away at college, I spent all of my time with Mike at his house. We developed a close relationship. He was very good to my daughter and extremely loving to my parents. He became the son they never had," says Yolanda.

"Over the years, his kindness extended to caring for my mom and dad, often driving them to medical appointments. His patience was astounding. One day, my father was scheduled for a check-up at St. John's Hospital in Queens, but it turned into a daylong event of test taking. Mike insisted that everything get completed that day, and he sat there patiently with his newspaper, tending to everyone's needs throughout the day. To my mother, he was amazing.

"His concern for my parents lasted all of his life. When my dad did pass, my mom asked Mike to be a pallbearer. By carrying the casket, he honored and served my dad one last time. My mom felt that because he supported my dad so much in life, he would be an appropriate pallbearer.

"Although we had considered having children for many years, it was not meant to be. His retirement gave him the freedom to live life to the fullest. I was still working and could not participate in all of his endeavors. Michael felt that he had to explore the world around him; it was almost a necessity that he had.

"My love for him never ceased. I believed that by supporting his choices, our love would grow, and it did. I knew this because we always remained so close. We always had a mutual love and respect for each other that I will always cherish," declared Yolanda.

Blackout: Where Were You When the Lights Went Out?

The dark and steamy summer of 1977 was filled with debauchery despite the chaos caused by a serial killer known as Son of Sam. Although everyone's conversation centered around the latest news on the terror he was causing, kids still hung out in parked cars and roamed the neighborhoods. Crime was at its highest level in years and the streets were more dirty than they were clean.

Mike and John Albano were hanging out with two female friends at the infamous *Sandbox* sharing a few beers. Meanwhile the rain clouds hovered over the city promising some imminent relief to the sweltering temperatures. But Con Edison's massive power grids were not able to withstand the four powerful bolts and shortly after 9:30 p.m. the lights began to flicker and within an hour the Big Apple was plunged into total darkness.

As always, most New Yorkers responded to the crisis with resilience. It brought out the best in so many people, whose primary concern was to help out in a time of need. They volunteered and directed traffic at intersections without traffic lights. It was extraordinary. Of course as human nature would have it, it also brought out the worse in people. Neighborhoods exploded in violence, stores were ransacked and burned. Brooklyn was ravaged by looters, who helped themselves to so much merchandise that the night was dubbed "Christmas in July." The police were out in force to handle situations, but there were simply not enough of them. Still, about 4,000 arrests were made during the blackout. Over 1,000 fires burned throughout the city, six times the average rate.

With illumination coming only from street cars, Mike decided that a ride to the beach might be a good idea. "I don't remember the ride in Bubbles' car, but I do remember that I woke up in a sand dune at the beach. I thought we were on the moon!" How they got home that night remains a mystery.

It was some 24 hours before power was finally restored. Mayor Abe Beame, local and state officials, and New Yorkers could not fathom how four lightning bolts could effectively cripple the nation's largest city. They accused Con Edison of gross negligence, while the utility company blamed the crisis on an Act of God.

"The next day, trying to remember what had happened, I asked Bubbles what made him take us to the beach? He looks at me with that deadpan look and says, 'How the f**k do I know, it seemed to be as good a place as any at the time.' That's all, so Bubbles and I spent the blackout of 1977 together at the beach with two girls! I wish I could remember more!" says his old pal John Albano.

No Fear
~ *Raymond Capodanno remembers*

"Over the years, Mike and I spent a lot of time together," said Raymond. "It was amazing how much territory we covered. From Hunter Mountain to Europe, it was always an adventure. I may have gotten Michael into a few situations that were a bit insane, but Mike, being the calm, collected, level-headed guy that he was, always got things under control.

"One particular situation that comes to mind was in a pool hall in Hunter Mountain, sometime in the 1980s in the middle of the night. It involved a bunch of the guys, Jimmy Herro, Sam Grillo, Fuji, and me. We stayed at a place, a rental without a kitchen. We called it the 'Men's Shelter.' We stayed on the weekends for the whole summer. A few times, we may have rearranged the walls.

"It was an Irish bar/pub restaurant in the day, but at night it was an afterhours pool hall – the only afterhours place around in the Tannersville/Hunter Mountain area. By afterhours, it was full of really intoxicated people and smoke, creating layers of clouds thick enough to cut with a knife.

"The pool table had been left unattended for a while, although without staking claim to it, certain individuals always believed it was theirs for the taking. I placed a few quarters on the edge, refreshed my drink, and went back to start a game. I grabbed the rack, set it down on the table, packed the balls tightly inside and lifted the rack. I began by breaking the balls and continued shooting. This guy comes over to us and declares, 'Hey, I was in the middle of a game.'

"I said, 'No one was playing a game. The table was empty for over twenty minutes, now I'm in the middle of a game,' and I continued to play.

"Without hesitation or concern that he wrecked my game, he declared, 'You're not playing anymore!'

"I went over to Michael and decided that we would have a little fun. There was never any fear in Michael. 'Alright, whatever,' Michael said. 'What are you getting me into? Am I going to have to hit anyone?' Michael didn't like hitting anyone, and he reserved that tactic only for when necessary.

"I waited for these guys to be in the middle of their game, and then I approached them with more bravado then brains and asked, 'How is your game going?' Then I wrecked their game. Michael sprang into action as soon as he saw I was in imminent danger. With one hand, he lifted each guy and flung him across the room. With one arm! It ended with me getting knocked around and getting a few scratches and Michael getting me out of there!

"I really wasn't worried because I knew how strong Michael was. My first experience with seeing this was when a bunch of guys went to Spruce Pond camping. I bought a red cooler with no handles, and I just couldn't carry this thing up the mountain. It was clumsy and heavy as hell. As I was struggling with it, Michael grabbed it from me, threw it on his shoulder and pulled it up the mountain, without breaking a sweat – like it was a feather.

"I also witnessed his strength when I made the mistake of was annoying Mike one night is a club in Brooklyn called *Pastels*. He warned me to stop – more than once. Fed up with me, he grabbed me by the throat and with a stiff arm; he lifted me until I was dangling from the sky. With one arm, I went right up. At first I laughed, but I quickly changed my tune and apologized to him. After all, I was immobilized. He made me promise to stop annoying him, and then he put me down," laughed Raymond.

A New Era--On the Job
~ *Gaspare Randazzo remembers*

The New York City of the late 1970's and early 1980's looked very different from the gentrified metropolis we know today. The Bowery, now lined with luxury apartments, housed much of the city's illicit activities, while drug dealers and prostitutes worked openly from Park Slope to Times Square. At the same time, crack and heroin infested the city, driving the crime rate even higher. Along with those problems came Industrial decline and economic stagnation, which led to a dramatic downturn for America's largest city.

On December 31, 1980, Times Square was illuminated in neon signs advertising 'Evita,' 'Annie,' Coca-Cola, and Midori liquor. Approximately 400,000 people crowded into New York's most famous plaza. Dozens of additional police officers were dispatched to patrol the hordes. A few minutes before midnight, in the midst of the crowd on 44th Street, a teenager stabbed an officer and lunged at another before being shot. Otherwise, the crowd was unusually calm.

At 11:58 pm, the entire city observed a moment of silence for the 55 hostages held at the American embassy in Tehran by radical supporters of the Ayatollah Khomeini and the Iranian Revolution. In somber moments many New Yorkers prayed for a better world, a year of peace and non-aggression ahead.

There was no doubt New York City itself was in crisis, a metropolis in near-chaos with few hopes for recovery. The crime rate was of epic proportions.

One month later, the NYPD would produce crime figures from 1980 that confirmed the most dismal estimates – over a quarter of a million reported crimes, almost 2,000 homicides and over 100,000 reported robberies. On the first day of 1981, most New Yorkers held a more cynical view, one that would grimly play out in the days ahead.

By 4 a.m. on January 1, the crowd in Times Square had mostly dispersed. Prostitutes and pimps had re-taken their places on Eighth Avenue and along the side streets and down on 42nd Street, the porn theaters were in full swing.

Twenty-five days later, two young men stood in the corridors of 1 Police Plaza – two men ready to be sworn into the New York City Police Academy. Two young men, who only a few months earlier, were among hundreds willing to tackle one of the fiercest challenges of their lives – New York City.

"It is January 26, 1981 and I am standing in the lobby among a sea of soon-to-be police officers to be sworn in and suddenly I spot my old friend 'Bubbles.' What was he doing there? We had hung out with each other just a few days earlier and no mention was made of Mike becoming a cop."

Face to face, the two twenty-three year-olds were equally stunned at seeing each other. "The first thing Mike does is put his finger to his lips to shush me and to warn me not to speak of our encounter and future plans to anyone. I understood. Becoming a cop was a big deal in the neighborhood and it meant that you would no longer be able to hang out with certain characters or even be associated with others. I understood the need for privacy and anonymity. People started treating you differently when they knew you were becoming a cop, and it wasn't always respected. Mike especially understood that and we both knew how important it was to distance ourselves from the past. Even though we had such short pasts behind us, it was the 70s", Gaspare Randazzo explained.

"But of course Mike had to take it to extremes. He made me promise him over and over again that I wouldn't tell anyone and he kept making me swear every night until the day he left the NYPD to became a fireman. Then he wanted everyone to know, because everyone loves a fireman!

"Of course, I remained a cop in a city that hated us. Mike was a good cop and I'm sure he liked the job, even though he didn't want anyone to know what he did during the day. I think he told people that he was going to school to become an ophthalmologist. I'm not sure if anyone believed him and years later, I found out his sister was actually an ophthalmologist, so I guess he had a plausible story if he wanted one.

"Even in the academy, Mike did something heroic and made the papers. On his way into the academy, he saved someone in trouble. For someone who didn't want attention, he was always in the spotlight. Even so, he would call me up every night and ask me if I had told anyone. Back then we had no cell phones, so you had to be home to get those calls. After I assured him his secret was safe, we discussed the job.

"At the academy, we were put into companies alphabetically, he was in B and I was in R. The best part would be when we were out together among our old friends, maybe hanging out at a bar in Bay Ridge. It was a bit suspicious. We both stood out with our crew cuts in a time when a lot of guys still had a lot of hair and were wearing it in a ponytail. But Mike stuck to his story. Mysterious Mike was explaining the extremely clean-cut look as a prerequisite to being in Ophthalmologist school. People believed him. Mike was a smart guy, and anything was possible. I stood by, laughing to myself. I know Mike was a nervous wreck, thinking I would blow his cover, but I never would. Mike was a good guy and I respected his privacy. I also knew his mom was cop, and a lot of friends didn't know that. Not only was a woman cop a rarity, to have your friend's mom be a cop was totally unheard of.

"Later on, I was surprised to find out that his dad was a cop and was in the 78 precinct, where I worked, even though I never had the opportunity to meet him. You'd think Mike might've mentioned it when he found out I worked there!" Gaspare recalls.

"Six months later, we were sworn in as police officers. It was a proud day for our families.

"On the job, Mike and I listened to the stories. By the 1980s, the job had changed as we heard from the veterans. It was not the same job that his father had in the 1950s and 60s.

"We went to work every day, flew to details, walked a foot post, sat on DOA's, hospitalized prisoners and EDP's, or rode in an RMP (Radio Motor Patrol). Police officers were taught how to handle almost every job without getting the "boss" involved. The Sergeants and Lieutenants were in charge and allowed to run the command as they saw fit. Collars were made for dollars, and the later in the shift you made a collar, the more overtime, which translated into dollars. Being on the job was a great feeling. We covered for each other, and became best friends with our partners. You didn't want to miss work because you didn't want to miss anything! That was the job. It was tough and the city was in bad times, but we loved it. Like many guys, Mike had his foot in both doors so when the FDNY called, he made the switch. When he became a fire-man everyone knew." Gaspare concluded.

"In 2015, I found out from Mike's mom that Michael did attend Optometrist School in NYC. He did not discuss it with anyone and only used it as a cover story for the Police Academy. It seemed that Michael hated making glasses and trying on frames over people's noses all day. It was a job he knew he could not tolerate; therefore it was a short-lived career!

Decisions, Decisions
~ Nicki Sirakides remembers

Michael did attend Optometrist School in New York City. He did not discuss it with anyone and only used it as a cover story for the Police Academy. It seemed that Michael hated making glasses and trying on frames over people's noses all day. It was a job he knew he could not tolerate; therefore it was a short-lived career! "I hate putting glasses on people's noses all day!" he told his mother, "This life is not for me."

Michael, like his mother and father, loved the NYPD, and was proud to wear the uniform. But like his father, he had also taken the test for the FDNY and was terribly torn when he was called by the FDNY. Seeking his mother's advice, he was told, "Michael, your father was in the same situation. He had taken the Fire Department test while he was a patrolman. When he was called, he turned it down. The years that followed were the Knapp Commission; life was very different for patrolmen. During those years, he often said that he wished he had taken the job with FDNY." (During the Knapp Commission, Patrolman Frank Serpico revealed corruption in the Police Department. As a result, field officers of the Internal Affairs division were created in all precincts and undercover informants were placed in precincts. It became very difficult and stressful for decent cops trying to make a living.)

Mike couldn't decide what to do. So he sought out an old friend to ask her opinion. Nicki Sirakides recalls, "Mike was torn. He had just gone through the Police Academy and he knew how proud his mother was that he had become a cop, but part of him had always wanted to be a fireman. I guess it is sort of every boy's dream. So, he looked at it from a different perspective. We were hanging out and, all of a sudden, he takes out two pictures, one of himself dressed as a cop and the other dressed as a fireman. He wanted to know which one he looked better as—a cop or a fireman. What could I say? He looked pretty handsome in both!

"Years later, I visited New York from California with my first son James during Christmastime. Mike was so happy that I could visit the firehouse and bring James, too. I guess he made the right decision because he was one happy fireman!

"I've been out of New York for almost 20 years. Many friends have come and gone since I moved to California, but one friend remained solid: Mike. If I called and said we were coming in on Tuesday, he'd be meeting us at *Skinflints* on Wednesday. We'd reminisce about the *Yes* concert that my girlfriend, Diane, and I attended at Madison Square Garden. We had nosebleed seats. Somehow Mike and his brother Tony had 5th row seats. The night before, he told me he would come and find us in the sky and bring us down to the bottom. I didn't think he would do it. Lo and behold, on that night on August 5, 1977, during their second song *"I've Seen All Good People,"* I see Mike climbing up the bleachers to get us! He took us back down and we sat with them in their seats. We were pretty, young chickies back then, so it was easy to squeeze two in a seat. That's the kind of guy he was, solid, loyal and loving. Miss you Mike. Thanks for great memories."

Europe with the Boys
~ Raymond Capodanno remembers

"When in Rome…"

"Michael and Sam met up with me in France and we went out looking for a hotel. We had our standards and although they weren't much, we did prefer a three-star hotel. When we had checked in to acceptable accommodations, Mike told us to set up house in the hotel, dropped off his k stuff and then he disappeared.

"When he returned, as usual, he had accumulated an entourage. He found a bunch of girls for us to hang out with on the beach. He also informed us that he had met the owner of a hot nightclub in town. He said we were invited there that night. The girls were impressed with Michael being a firefighter. They kept addressing him as Pompier, Pompier!

Without going into too many details, a small fire ignited when a sheer scarf was tossed over a lampshade. Needless to say, the material heating up and ignited. The crazy girl couldn't stop yelling "Pompier, Pompier!" Once again, Mike had to save the day. I'm not sure it was what he had in mind. After that incident, we weren't sure what to expect when we went out that night.

"We managed to find the hot spot of French nightlife where Mike had procured us an invitation. Sure enough, when we arrived we went to the front of the line where Michael and his new friend, the owner, exchanged hugs and handshakes. We got right in," recalled Raymond.

The French were known for their all-day parties. They get started in the morning and go past midnight, and then they convert into after-hour clubs. The crowd was young and international so the guys fit right in. It was a trendy, edgy spot to hang until seven in the morning, just about when they re-opened for the all-day long party.

"In Monaco, which is famed for its glamour, wealth, and blue waters of the Mediterranean, we were truly the ugly Americans because of our coolers, alcohol, blankets, and American ways. We were driving along the highway, spending a half a day looking for a cooler, finally settling for a makeshift plastic pail with a bag full of ice. Michael was getting all anxious in the back seat and tossed a small piece of trash out the window. Of course, we get pulled over. We are told that we are going too slowly and that throwing trash out the window constitutes a fine payable by cash. The cops showed us the manual and let us know we are in trouble. Somehow between Mike and me, we managed to talk him out of it and convinced him he was a "cool cop;" he let us go without a fine!" remarked Raymond.

While in Marseilles, the second largest city in France, Michael was able to find Marins-Pompiers (sailor-firefighters) who provide their fire and rescue services for the city. He had brought over American shirts, hats, and pins and traded with them for firefighter products from Marseilles.

"In 1989, Michael and a friend of mine, Kim, from Atlanta, Georgia came to visit me in Italy again," says Raymond. "For some reason, Kim attracted a lot of attention. She was a very cool-looking American. We all decided to take a gondola ride. Kim was a little disappointed because we were in the perfect romantic setting and none of us were involved with each other. She had to settle for the beautiful sights of Venice for the 40-minute ride with the dolce tones of the gondolier gliding along the Grand Canal.

"In 2004, Michael and I found ourselves back in France where he had a chance to meet my extended family. He met my father's sister's husband, Lorenzo, who is an interesting man. Lorenzo was a member of the French resistance during WWII. Michael had a fascination with WWII history and memorabilia. We went to visit a flea market in a small village that was housed in the rubble of an edifice. Michael bought old artwork, newspaper, German paraphernalia; it was such a thrill for him. Mike and Lorenzo spoke to each other for hours on end about the resistance.

"He shared stories of how, when with the French Resistance, he played a vital part in aiding the Allies to success in Western Europe – especially leading up to D-Day in June 1944. The French Resistance supplied the Allies with vital intelligence reports as well as doing a huge amount of work to disrupt the German supply and communication lines within France. Michael was fascinated with my uncle's stories.

"When Lorenzo's daughter, Michella, and her husband and kids came to visit America, Michael remembered their outdoor oven pizza parties and how hospitable they were. He was able to really show them a good time in the United States," remembers Raymond.

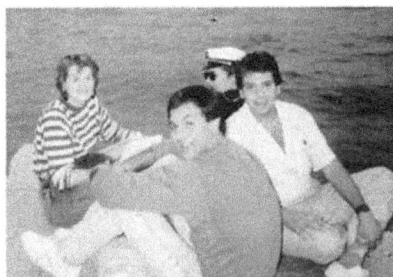

(Top Left) Mike, Ray Capodanno and Kim in Rome
(Top Right) Mr. and Mrs. Capodanno, Mike and Kim, Abbey of
San Michele Arcangelo (Middle and Bottom) Venice, 1988

I Read the News Today. Oh Boy!

On January 22, 1997 *The New York Times*, *The Daily News* and local Brooklyn Newspapers reported the following story: *Bensonhurst Blaze Injures 7. Elderly Man and Woman are Critical.*

The blaze occurred in Bensonhurst on West 8th Street between Avenue O and Avenue P. The elderly couple was taken to the New York Hospital-Cornell Medical Center Burn Unit. The two-alarm fire burned fiercely on both floors of the two-story, four-apartment brick house. According to the Fire Department, Mike Behette of Ladder Co. 172 arrived and spotted the elderly woman at an upstairs window.

"She was at the window and screaming," Mike said, "She almost jumped in my arms. I took her down (the ladder) with one arm holding her and one arm on the ladder." On the way down, the woman told Mike that her sister was on the second floor. Mike turned her over to the medics and dashed back up the ladder without hesitation. Once inside, Mike and Patrick Klein of Ladder Co. 156 carried her through the interior stairs. Three police officers suffered smoke inhalation and minor burns, and a firefighter sustained a burn to his chest. A dog was also rescued from the second floor. It had apparently sought refuge in a corner closet where firefighters found it.

"All in a day's work," Mike would say.

Two Mikes
~ *MIKE BESIGNANO REMEMBERS*

The two Mike B's had so much in common, including the fact that they had both previously been New York City police officers. It was a popular way to begin a Civil Service career in New York. Although both men were single at the time, Mike Behette liked to give Mike Besignano relationship advice, always beginning with, "Hey, you're the second best-looking guy in the firehouse," remembers Besignano. "He said it every time he saw me, like it was my name. It never got old. He was a very private guy, very quiet– a gentle giant. But one thing was for sure: we knew he loved his mom. He was a great son," says Besignano.

"Another thing Mike loved was Brooklyn. The guys would get together before checks every week. Mike was always there – there wasn't much that he missed. Being single, he didn't have a wife or kids, so he did what he wanted. He loved Brooklyn. When I complained about Brooklyn because there was no place to park, he'd say, "What are you kidding? I love Brooklyn! Nothing bothered him about it. He had such a passion for it," remembers Mike.

A fire department works as a team. These team members are specially trained and equipped to enter burning buildings, chop holes in the roof to let smoke escape, and rescue anyone who might still be inside. Each team member has a role. For example, the Fire Engine Chauffeur drives the ladder truck to the fire scene, and once there, the chauffeur is responsible for controlling the water pump, raising and positioning the ladder and bucket, then removing trapped occupants from the front of the building. An Engine Chauffeur is also accountable for all the equipment on the rig, checking the engines and making sure any damage is repaired. This was the position Mike chose.

The tower-ladder has a bucket platform at the end of it. From the bucket, firefighters can rescue people or spray water from air directly into the burning building.

"Mike was a giant man who didn't know his own strength. I have seen him take doors out that you needed two guys for and he's just go there and take it off. Boom! The door was open and you were in.

"We had a 95-foot ladder; it was 20 feet longer than the regular ones. I was up in the bucket, they would special call us a lot, to go higher and pour water on the roofs, so we'd be up in the bucket for an hour or two. That's where Mike gave me advice about women. He gave me some crazy advice about how women think and how to date! This was all before my wife," remembers Mike.

"I lived in Staten Island and we would get detailed. Mike called and asked me to switch a detail. Someone brought my gear home and I worked in Staten Island, right by my house. Mike worked Brooklyn. That night they had a serious fire in a two-story attached house. Mike recued a lady, and then they found another guy unconscious on the 2nd floor. That night, they saved a few peoples' lives. I think that was great. I was a little upset that I missed it, but that's the nature of the job!

"The next day, I was working in Brooklyn, finishing my 24-hour tour. That night after the fire, we went back and critiqued the fire. Apparently, the family of the older woman and the other victims were there. A woman started asking, "Where's Mike? Where's Mike?" One of the guys pointed to me. She darted over and started hugging me, thinking I was Mike Behette. I told her, 'I'm Mike, but I'm not Mike Behette. But I'll relay your hugs to him. He'll really appreciate it.' It was nice. Probably a fire he would always remember.

"He always called me after I left the job. You work with some guys and they are acquaintances, but not Mike. When I retired, he was probably one of the three guys that kept in touch with me. I appreciated that a lot about him. It's amazing how many friends you make over the years and then in the end, it's only a few that remain loyal. One of those guys was Mike.

"Now I have a different life in Florida. My kids get to see me. I retired in 2006. I was in my third year as a lieutenant. We were at a serious fire on Staten Island. After all the instances I heard about guys getting sick, I decided to walk away while I was still well. After a trip to Disney World, we decided to relocate in Florida.

"When I heard Mike got sick, I said, 'It's always the really good guys. Another good friend, Johnny Graziano – the Big Dog – is also sick. He has pancreatic cancer. Another great guy."

"I don't understand how I got this," Behette told his pal Mike over and over. All he could say was, "Mike, we're firemen. It could've been 9/11. We were in fires, asbestos. Could be so many things we were exposed to." Mike didn't even smoke, remembers Besignano.

"We had weekly softball games and threw around a lot of darts. During the ballgames, he always hit the ball to right field. It was the strangest thing – only right field. It was a championship game for our battalions and Mike was up. We all knew it. Mike was going to hit the ball to right field. Right field it was! It was a winner. He won the game. He was the hero of that day. It was great," remembers Mike B., the second best-looking guy at the station.

Brother Firefighters and friends

Keeping Us Connected
~ *Brian DiSanti remembers*

> *"Individual commitment to a group effort—
> that is what makes a team work, a company
> work, a society work, a civilization work."*
>
> ~Vince Lombardi

B rian DiSanti, an old friend, was asked to say a few words about Mike. His first reaction was that he couldn't just say a "few" words about Mike because he was a guy that you just couldn't say enough about. But he gave it a try.

"When you look back, it is hard to believe how time goes by. It was over thirty years ago that a bunch of young kids, all in their early twenties, were assigned as probies to the Bensonhurst firehouse of Engine 330/Ladder 172.

"We were all just starting our careers and, basically, our adult lives. As each individual navigates his way through his career, as in life, change is inevitable.

"Some guys transfer to other boroughs closer to home, some to busier companies, and some get promoted and have to leave their firehouse. As you say goodbye to your buddies, you meet new comrades and begin to cultivate relationships with them.

"But there are always those few guys that remain the constants in your career and ultimately when you retire, they remain the constants in your life. To so many – at least to the fortunate – that guy was Mike."

Crediting Mike with keeping everyone in touch with each other, Brian DiSanti said, "There were a few of us that moved out of state after retirement, but because of Mike, we were never out of touch with one another. Whenever I would call him from Florida to see how he was doing, he would say, 'Hey, I'm with so-and-so. Say hello.' And he would hand the phone over. If one of us out-of-towners was in town visiting, Mike would set up a dinner and get all of us together.

"Mike spent his entire career in E-330/L-172 in Bensonhurst and he was quite content with that. He helped bridge the gap between the new guys coming on and the senior guys in the house. Every firehouse needs a guy like Mike to pass on the tradition of the job and to set the tone of the firehouse. Mike was the guy who kept everyone connected. John Graziano nicknamed him "Elmer" because he was the glue that held us all together!

"Every couple of months or so, Mike would make calls and organize some sort of reunion or get together so we could all catch up with one another. When Mike called, you felt obligated to him to show up because he would put so much effort into it. If you made excuses about why you couldn't come, he would just say, 'If you're here, you're here. If not, you're not.'

"I would marvel at his ability to organize these blessed events in such record time. He would also delegate you to call other people. He wanted everyone present! I would take a step back and watch as he would relish in the fact that he got us all together. He would be like a proud parent and we were his kids."

Mike had a passion for the Army–Navy Game. Every year he purchased about 30 tickets and enjoyed going with his buddies. Another one of his passions was the New York Jets. It was at these games that Mike merged his Fire Department friends and his old buddies from the Bay Ridge neighborhood.

A FISH STORY
~ JIM SECHIANO L-172 (1990-2001)

"L-172 and Engine-330 had a fishing trip early one morning. Mike showed up after a long night out and was extremely tired. We all entered a contest to see who would catch the biggest fish. Mike paid his $10.00 entry fee, put his fishing line in the water (I don't know if he even put bait on the hook), and immediately went to sleep in the boat's cabin. At the end of the trip, the boats captain called for the lines to be pulled up so we could head back to shore. Everyone who had caught a fish took their biggest one to the back of the boat to see who had won the contest.

"The captain called out, 'We can't leave because one line is still in the water.' That is when we realized Mike was still sleeping in the cabin, so we told him to pull up his line. Mike got up (a little upset that he was disturbed) and reeled in his line with the biggest fish of the day on the end – hooked in the tail, with no bait!" laughed Jim.

"One of the many great things about Mike was he made you smile, always living life to the fullest. Out of the blue, he would call you from Lourdes, France and ask if you need any Holy Water or from South Beach, Florida because he couldn't remember a name and hoped you could help him. You never knew where he would show up, from pictures with Sir Paul McCartney, Bill Clinton and Rudy Giuliani, to being interviewed on TV by Larry King," Jim reminisced.

My Pal
~ Patrick Corbett remembers

"Why is it," he said, one time, at the subway
entrance, "I feel I've known you so many years?"

"Because I like you," she said, "and I
don't want anything from you."

~ Ray Bradbury, Fahrenheit 451

"My friend, Mike, or as Mike would always call you – Pal. Yes, he certainly was a true pal indeed. Always up for doing different things and going to different places and events. I believe I first met Mike in the local bar *Bennett's* through some mutual friends. I really don't remember the exact first encounter, but once I started talking to Mike, more and more I could see he would be a person of interest for me to hang with," remembers Patrick.

"And then of course, once I saw he loved to do things and go places like I did and he hardly drank at all and was willing to drive, well, needless to say, it was True Love! That's just a joke (sort of)—I mean, Mike driving was nice but it went well beyond that.

"Mike would always say, 'You drive there and I will drive home. We will go there, stay a few hours, and then come home' What can I say? 'Sounds good, Mike.' However, the only staying a few hours part did not always happen. Yeah, we pushed it to the limits some nights, staying till closing, etc.

"I mean, as expected, there were some arguments at times, like telling us to lower the radio, asking us if we really need to go to the diner, or simply walking around the bar trying to gather us all up to finally leave for home, saying, 'Didn't you guys drink enough?' I have to say, Mike was a great sport about it all, putting up with our shit! But hey, that's what pals sometimes do to each other. And you could see he was also enjoying the night.

"Mike would always kid around the next day, saying things like, 'You have the Irish flu, Pat' or joking, saying 'I wish I could be like you guys to be able to drink and eat so much.' One time Mark replied, 'Fine, if you want to be like us, when you wake up in the morning, bang your head against the wall, drink a cup of sand, and dump your wallet down the toilet. Then you will be just like us!' He got a good laugh out of that, as he did with most of our other escapades.

"It was a pleasure having him as our friend, but more of a pleasure being allowed into his world. Mike was a private, quiet type of person, so I felt it was a Big Privilege to be one of his pals he let in.

"Mike, as we all know, was not the most patient person," laughed Patrick. "We would say to him, 'Mike, you are always in a hurry to get somewhere so you can leave. You see, when you are true pals, you can mess with one another, laugh, and play jokes on each other. Some good old friendly abuse amongst friends.

"I said to Mike one day, 'Let's make a pact. Seeing we both enjoy going to different places and keeping busy, then whenever one of us has something planned, always let the other one know about it. If you can make it, great; if not, at least you knew about it. After the first trip, I am glad Mike continued to involve me in his plans.

"On a nice Wednesday afternoon in the summer, Mike, Kevin, and I decided to head to the Jersey Shore. Yes, me and Kevin proceeded to enjoy a bunch of drinks on the beach while Mike relaxed with the paper. Then a few more with some lunch. Then we asked Mike if we could stay to go to club at night, and he said yes. Once we got in the club, that was it. We were having a great time. We lost sight of each other at one point, then finally (right around closing) Mike said it was time to leave. Of course, we had some pizza first, then got into the truck. Radio blasting, we were ready to enter the highway. Local or express were our choices. 'Express, Express' was being slurred from the back seat and from me as well, so Mike went that route. Soon into it was bumper-to-bumper traffic while the local side was wide open. Then, a car sped by on local side, and I said to Kevin, 'Wow, he must have been doing 70-80 mph. If he lives in Brooklyn, he will be home in about 30 minutes.' Oh Man! Mike let out such a huge sigh. Yeah, true pals can really mess with each other.

"Mike was a HUGE Beatles fan, and we were all excited about seeing Ringo Starr in concert in Manhattan. Mike, his brother Tony, and I went. Next door to the venue was a bar where and Tony and I proceeded to drink, while Mike was pacing around saying, 'Guys, we really need to stand on line.' The concert was general admission, so Mike wanted the stage. 'Mike, don't worry about it, we have plenty of time,' we said. After more pacing, and me and Tony ordering another round, Mike panicked and left for the line. We finally go in (before the concert started) and there was plenty of room in the rear by the bar to drink and dance. Tony talked to Micky Dolenz from The Monkees for a little bit, and Mike was in his glory, dancing around in front of the stage. It was a great night!

"Whenever Mike and I would go out together, I understood him not wanting to just stand at the bar while I drank, and he didn't. That didn't interest him for the entire evening. So yeah, he would leave temporarily for walks or to get something to eat and eventually return, so it was all good. We knew what we liked and we both wanted to be there, but enjoying some of the moments was done differently. It was nice though, knowing we were able to do that. We understood what each of us liked. And then sometimes I would tell Mike before leaving on a trip, I was bringing along a buffer – another friend to fill in while he walked around. He got a kick out of that – but I did do it a few times," remembers Patrick.

"Yeah, there were many trips and outings I was fortunate to share with my pal, Mike. Some he introduced to me, that he shared and invited me on, and some I shared with him. A few of the ones we did together that he really loved were:

- Jersey Shore/Annual Dunes Day at Donovan's Reef in Sea Bright. Bands would play all day and night until closing. You set up in your spot on the beach, eat and drink, and swim and listen to all the bands play. Mike really enjoyed this day from the first time I took him. After that, every summer, he would always ask me what date it was on.
- Buena Sera Bar in Red Bank, NJ. We used to go there a lot after the summer for drinks and dancing. A lot of fun and Mike was almost always in for that night out.
- Annual Army/Navy Game in Philadelphia. The first time I went with Mike, it was him, Yolanda, and I. There was a blizzard the night before and the next morning he called me saying, 'I guess we are not going. I just got my new pick-up truck so I said, 'Mike, we are going.' So, thankfully, we made it after a tough drive. What a cold day, but we stayed for the entire game. Mike loved all the pre-game festivities and on this day, Mike was talking to this old-timer before the game who has been going to this game for a very long time. Mike loved his stories; he really enjoyed speaking to this man about the history of this game. Yes, he made sure we always left in plenty of time in the morning because he truly enjoyed all the pre-game festivities.
- Veterans Day Parade in Manhattan – Mike loved parades, in general. Besides the Super Bowl parade for Giants, this I believe was the only other parade I went to with Mike. I never used to go to it before. But when I did for the first time, being a veteran myself, it was really nice. And Mike was like a little kid for everything that passed us by.

- I never really saw Mike go into the water on the beach outings, etc. so not sure if he really liked it or not. It definitely seemed that way when I invited him out on a friend's boat one weekend day. We had a bunch of boats head out to this island where you can dock up, walk around, and go swimming. This is an all-day event, which I thought I explained to Mike. Anyway, not going in the water or drinking like everyone else, Mike was starting to feel very ready to get back to land. However, no boats were returning to dock just yet. The sun was out and no one was near ready to leave. At one point, he was sitting on the front of the boat with his legs hanging over the edge and his chin resting on his hands, staring out. And in the distance we saw a water taxi boat. So Mike was thinking he would take that to the area (on land) that we were planning on going to next (this bar we were going to by boat). Then he would just meet us there. At least he would be off the boat. But the water taxi never really got close enough. Then, another one of Mike's favorite band's (The Rolling Stones) song, *I Can't Get No Satisfaction*, came on, so we all started to dance around near Mike singing, "I can't get no – Water Taxi" and of course kept singing that as the chorus. I think he laughed, don't remember, but we all did! I'll say it again: True Pals are the ones you can mess with.

"It was a pleasure experiencing some of these life events with my pal Mike and I know I left out a bunch more. I miss them very much," Patrick continued. "There have been so many since he left us that I know he would have loved to be a part of. It was a privilege being allowed into his world. Mike, you are missed every day. Thank you for sharing in parts of my life. We will meet again – just not now. Until then, Cheers!!!"

The Clan
~ Nicholas Walsh remembers

Aristotle said, "My best friend is the man who in wishing me well, wishes it for my sake."

In that sense, Mike was a best friend to so many. He truly wished you the best. To be a friend of Mike was almost like being in his clan. He made sure friends were friends with each other.

Nicholas Walsh remembers that when he met Greg, they became best of friends. Greg introduced him to Brian, and then Brian introduced him to Mike Behette. That's when he realized he had become part of an extended family.

"Although I considered Greg and Brian as my family, it wasn't until Mike that I realized the extent of the family they belonged to. Anyone who knew Mike knew him in a special place. He and I would discuss astrology. Well, it was more like Mike explaining to me how I always meet women that were a match for him and he always met women that were a match for me.

"Brian would come from Florida to visit and always got a group of us together for dinner and laughs. One night Mike asks him "How come you always make the plans?" Brian responded by telling Mike to make the plans next time.

"Sure enough, the next time Brian came into New York, Mike made the plans. I got a text from him saying, 'We're meeting Brian at Z-One in Staten Island for dinner…Be there at 7…Ok? Mike'

"When I got there and saw the guys, our usual crowd of 8-10 guys, I was told that everyone in the place was a friend of Mike's! Shocked that he knew all these people, someone asked him how it happened. His reply, 'When I ask people to show-up, they SHOW-UP!'

"I am glad a book was written about a man who made me his friend and changed my life in many ways. He was profound and simple, extremely smart and clumsy, but he was your friend, you were the second best looking guy in the room!" recalls Nicholas Walsh.

FIELD OF DREAMS
– TONY BEHETTE REMEMBERS

"One of the best stories to share about my brother Mike Behette was his generosity. Mike had a friend, Louie, who told Mike that he could get tickets to the 2000 Mets – Yankees World Series. The deal was that you could get a face value Upper Deck ticket for $110. The catch was that you had to use the Highland ferry as the way to get to Yankee Stadium (at a round trip ticket cost of $140) from the Highlands in New Jersey. Mike said he wanted to take his nieces, 11 year-old Danielle and 9 year-old Allison to the Subway Series of our lifetime," Tony remembered.

"Mike bought four tickets each for Games 1, 2, and 6. The opening day of the World Series was Saturday, October 21, 2000. The fourth ticket went to Louie. They had to be on the ferry by 6 o'clock to be in time for the 8 o'clock start, so they left Bay Ridge at 4:30 to get to the ferry. I remember telling them that we would be waiting by the 69th Street Pier to see them passing. Cellphones were not as plentiful as they are today. Mike had one and we had one for our family. I told the girls to call me so that we can catch a glimpse of them on the ferry. As they passed the 69th Street Pier, we were conversing about the enthusiasm of going to THE BIG GAME.

Game 1 was really one for the books, lasting 5 hours for a total of 12 innings. It wasn't until a Yankees walk-off single, well after 1 a.m., that they departed in great spirits – Yankees fans that they were!

The energy from the high of a Yankees win quickly dissipated; as it was now well after both of his nieces' bedtimes. The ferry ride, which was about 90 minutes, did not leave until an hour after the game ended, so they did not even reach Mike's car until around 3:30 a.m.

Maryann and I had watched the game at our friend's house and went to sleep by 1:30 a.m. sometime around 5 a.m.; Maryann nudged me to ask if the girls are home yet. I said I didn't know and went to check. I came back and said, 'Not yet.' 'Well,' Maryann said in disbelief, 'what do you mean they're not home?' and proceeded to call Mike's cellphone. Danielle, apparently woken up by the phone, answered. Maryann asked her where they were and Danielle stated that she didn't know but it looked like they were on a highway. When Maryann asked to speak to Michael, she was informed that he was talking to a cop on the side of the road. That's right; Mike got pulled over by the cops for speeding. What were the odds? Well, as anyone who was ever a passenger in his car knew, probably about 1 to 5.

The next morning, Allison told us that, not only was Mike pulled over for speeding, but that he was out talking to the cop for 20 minutes! (Mike later assured us that it was more like five minutes.) Apparently, when Mike showed his trusty FDNY badge, he found out that the cop, like most cops, really wanted to be a firefighter and had a lot of questions about the job. Mike, wanting to get out of a ticket, answered all his questions and continued a conversation with him and of course, successfully avoided the ticket. By the time the made it home, it was 5:30 a.m. What excitement for these girls!

The next day, Sunday, October 22, 2000, my mom told us that the Patriarch to the Melkite Church was saying Mass at the Church of the Virgin Mary that morning and would love for the girls and us to be there. After the Mass, there would be a luncheon at the Rex Manor. Mom never asked for anything, so I told the girls that this was a must, even though they were exhausted from the game the previous night. Maybe they were still riding on the adrenaline from the baseball game, but the girls managed to attend the event and even stay awake for all of it.

That same Sunday night, Mike, Louie, Yolanda and I went to Game 2 of the Subway Series– only this time, we learned from our mistake. We had Louie meet us at Yankee Stadium with the tickets rather than taking what my girls dubbed 'the slow boat to China.' Once again, it was an exhilarating game that the Yankees won. Instead of extra innings, the excitement came from the controversy surrounding Roger Clemens allegedly throwing a shattered bat at Mike Piazza. It was a long night and everyone was tired, but the sports weekend wasn't over quite yet.

The next night, Monday, October 23, the Jets were playing the Dolphins at home for Monday Night Football. Not wanting to give up our tickets, Mike, Yolanda, my friend Mary Griffin, and I went to the game after work. Changing gears from baseball to football was as easy for Mike as changing speeds from 50mph to Warp Factor 2. This talent would come in handy on a historic night in the fall of 2000.

Miami Dolphins, aka "the Fish," started the 4th quarter with a lead of 30-7. Mike, probably exhausted from the previous two nights, said, 'This game was over at the half. Let's get out of here.'

Now, leaving a Monday night blowout game early is acceptable, as long as it's not too early. It's one of those unwritten rules everyone just knows. As our convoy of miserable Jets fans hits the parking lot, those fumbling bumbling Jets score a TD, but miss the two-point conversion. 'They still suck.'

We hit Route 3 as the Jets hit the end zone again! Down 10 points with lots of time left, Mike starts repeating non-stop, 'I'll never leave a game early again.' A voice from the back seat was heard stating, 'I would never leave early, but it's not my car.' Now driving angry, Mike is doing about 90mph. The New Jersey Turnpike was our private runway as we rapidly approach takeoff speed! Thank goodness for gravity! Our goal now was *Bennett's Pub* on Ft. Hamilton Parkway – the home of the world's smallest big screen TV and an oasis for Jets fans. The normal wall of Staten Island traffic had dissolved into the night air. Sparks shot out from the undercarriage as we set the record for bottoming out that still stands today. Mike does a classic 'Starsky & Hutch' tire-screeching park in front of the almost abandoned *Bennett's*. Muffled cheering can be heard as Jumbo Elliott pretends the football is a cheeseburger and scores on a tackle-eligible pass. We got there to see the replay of the Jumbo Elliot three-yard completion from Vinny Testeverde for a touchdown to tie the game at 37. We then watched the rest of the game, including overtime, and the Jets won on a 40-yard field goal from John Hall. In obvious shock, all Mike would say that night was, 'I'll never leave a game early again.'

THE ATTACK, THE AFTERMATH, THE PILE

"You can be sure that the American spirit
will prevail over this tragedy."

- COLIN POWELL

In 1971, when the second tallest building in the world was erected, no one could imagine that it would one day become the target for mass destruction. Michael Behette and thousands of others lost too many brothers during the September 11, 2001 terrorist attacks, and as a horrified nation sat glued to the television for days, Michael plowed through the wreckage.

The morning of Sept. 11, 2001 began like any other Tuesday for many people. The Twin Towers stood tall in the Financial District as they had for more than 30 years. Michael had been enjoying the warmth and brightness of Florida sunshine on a well-deserved vacation cruise, possibly still asleep at 8:46 a.m. when American Airlines Flight 11 crashed into the North Tower of New York City's World Trade Center.

As the world debated about what had just happened, United Airlines Flight 175 zoomed in and this time crashed into the South Tower of the world famous high-rise, erasing any suspicions of pilot error and revealing it for what it was– a terrorist attack against the United States of America. Although it was hit second, the South Tower was first to collapse at 9:59 a.m. The North Tower fell at 10:28 a.m. It took less than 30 seconds for the Towers to fall.

By then, Michael knew that his cruise was over. He jumped ship with just the clothes on his back and his wallet, rented a car and made his way back from a vacation in Florida. With no formulated plan, he drove all day and through the night from Florida to the smoldering ruins of the World Trade Center.

As in most households, the Behette's home was flooded with phone calls asking where Michael was. "Michael is in Florida on a cruise, thank the Lord, thank the Lord," his mother told friends and loved ones over and over. Madeleine was grateful Michael was away. If he had not been, she was certain his image would've have flashed across the screens along with the other 343 firefighters and paramedics and 60 police officers who rushed to help and didn't make it out.

His cousin Jennifer Hayek remembers, "On 9/11, like everyone else, we were in a panic. I had been away at college and for three days no one from my family could contact Mikey. All we kept hearing about were all the terrible deaths and we knew Mikey would be there with his company if it was happening in New York. The cell service was down into New York City. We were so relieved to find out he was okay. Mike wasn't home; he was in Florida. Little did we know, he was racing to Ground Zero to help all those who weren't okay. He raced so fast he got a speeding ticket! Little did we know this would happen as a result. I thought that was one of the worst days of my life—wondering where he was, and was he safe. But the worst day was when he died."

But, as it was happening all Michael had were radio announcements from the rented car he drove way above the speed limit to get back to New York.

Most radio shows were doing their small talk thing when the first airplane hit the Twin Tower but they dropped the regular format and began relaying information from news sources. Many of the NYC stations had witnesses the second strike and collapse of the south tower and had to evacuate for their own safety. What was most frightening for New Yorkers was the thought that more attacks would hit the city. Michael rushed home with these thoughts in his mind – thoughts of his mother, brother, sister, and their families, thought of his brothers in the FDNY, who he knew would be among the first responders.

Listening to the radio, his only source of information, Mike wept as heard all types of reports, and tried to sort out facts from the many rumors that were spinning out of control, rumors like that there were thirteen more planes headed for New York City. He was in a vulnerable situation; there wasn't enough information for anyone to fully comprehend what was occurring. All he had to go on was his intuition and his willingness to listen to his gut, and his gut told him to get back to New York City. Michael often spoke about how painful it was for him to hear all the news secondhand on the radio; he cried his way back home. Yet, nothing could prepare him for what he saw.

In the chaotic days following the attack, he made his way to what became known as *The Pile* and spent the next few months working alongside his brothers, emergency responders, and volunteers as they sifted through debris, hoping to find survivors. Part of what they did was pass buckets back and forth, hour after hour, and every once in a while they asked for quiet when they thought they heard someone.

When he could speak about it, Mike shared some of the grueling details. He explained how they had to look through the debris and crawl through the spaces that were void, yet scattered with the dust and bones – mostly shattered – of human remains. The teams used listening devices and cameras attached to long poles to search in between the cracks and crevasses where rescue workers couldn't fit.

During the rescue mission, thousands of men and women were on *The Pile* sifting through the debris for survivors, or in most cases, remains. "At times, it seemed like mass confusion," admitted Mike. "It was good that everyone would help, but there were drawbacks too."

During those early days, The National Guard brought the military capacity for moving personnel and materials to the army of volunteers and emergency responders. Within days, fences went up—thousands of feet of chain-link that cut the neighborhood in half. From Chambers Street toward Rector Street, and from Broadway to the West Side Highway, was the *Frozen Zone* and there was strict control over that area. No one but officials passed through; soldiers with automatic weapons made sure of that. But even north of the *Zone*, life as we'd known it had ceased.

Working at *Ground Zero* meant no access to cell phone service, and in many cases, land lines. Duties were divided among firefighters, who handled the site of the attack; the military, who handled the security and organization of personnel in a radius around *Ground Zero*; and the police, who handled everything else. Troops of Marines and the New York Naval Militia were on duty for security in the area. Contractors had to be checked in and out of secured areas. They moved personnel and equipment for emergency personnel. They organized the volunteers and responders into units and restored some degree of normalcy to the channels of operation.

Mike described it as being chaotic at first. It was difficult to follow the channels of command and communication in the midst of such turmoil and carnage. Despite the EMT's efforts to give medical attention, little was needed. Moments after the plane hit, people started appearing at the edge of the buildings. The raging fire inside had made them make the most irrational decision of their lives. People began attempting to climb out onto the structure of the building to get away from the intense heat and unfortunately were ultimately forced to jump. A decision to jump from 70 stories in the air was one made out of sheer desperation and hopelessness. Some held hands with colleagues; some wrapped their arms around each other as they stepped together into empty air. The Towers were originally built with a helicopter landing pad, so some may have hoped to be lifted off the roof, but there was no way out. Access to the roof was locked, and even if the helipad was in working order, the dense smoke would have prevented any rescue effort from the roof. At the base of the building people stood and watched as desperate men and women dropped in front of them. Those outside the building caught in showers of burning fuel on the sidewalk were rushed to Weil

Cornell Medical Center for treatments, but few survived. History had taught us that during the Triangle Shirtwaist Factory fire, some who briefly survived after having jumped from windows claimed they had done so to be sure their bodies would be identified, not obliterated in the fire.

Mike may have expected to see the furnishings of an office – computers, desks, etc., but instead what they all saw was just a heap of dust — crushed fire trucks and ambulances, paper still floating through the air filling every crevice. Nothing, other than steel, was recognizable. It was all one big heap– *The Pile.*

Unfortunately, there were not many survivors to find. Mike and the others *Ground Zero* volunteers had the heartbreaking mission to sift carefully through the debris in search of human remains. Under unstable fallen buildings, engineers worried that the weight of trucks and cranes would cause the wreckage to shift and collapse again, so the workers used bucket brigades instead. Meanwhile, huge fires continued to burn at the center of *The Pile.* Jagged, sharp pieces of iron and steel were everywhere. Around him, Michael could see that many firefighters and police officers wrote their names and phone numbers on their forearms in case they fell into the hole or were crushed.

Mike knew that among the almost 3,000 people that lay there were his buddies. All he wanted to do was help. While removing piles of debris hour after hour, he didn't consider that he was putting his own safety at risk, neither did so many others. If he did think about it, he was nonetheless compelled to risk his own well-being to save and honor others. After all, Michael was a firefighter, doing what he was trained to do: help others in need. On *The Pile* Mike experienced an extreme camaraderie despite despicable circumstances. Everyone was there for a common goal. Mike didn't have time to think much about what he was doing, he just did it.

It Just Wasn't Enough
– Dr. Marguerite Behette remembers

It's hard to imagine that a generation of children have grown up since the 9/11 attacks, and for them, the incidents were as foreign as World War II was to Michael's generation. Yet for some, the reality remains alive in the recounting of stories from family members who lived, breathed, and paid the ultimate price of that devastating day.

Dr. Marguerite Behette remembers volunteering, first at the hospitals, and then at the site. Of course, there were so few survivors needing assistance that her efforts were guided elsewhere in the rescue efforts. It was during those days when the alarm would sound at Ground Zero, that Dr. Behette would brace herself in the direction of the sound. Following the crowd, she knew the alarm was a signal for a beam or structure on the verge of a collapse, or perhaps a diesel fuel tank that had been buried seven stories below presented the risk of explosion.

Despite the fact that approximately 500 amateur radio operators volunteered their services during the discovery and recovery efforts to maintain communications, Dr. Behette worried about the rescue workers. She worried about the men and women working without proper respirators to protect them against toxins such as airborne asbestos. Many were wearing only a painter's mask; some had no facial covering at all. Dr. Behette watched as the fearless men and women made due with skimpy masks and sometimes a bottle of Vicks Vapor Rub to mask the wretched odors. She watched as they removed whatever minimal protection they had, every time they stopped to have a bite to eat. It was a surreal, worrisome experience. But most of all, she worried about one special firefighter who gave it his all without concern for himself – her brother, Michael Behette.

Like Forrest Gump
~ Mike Besignano remembers

*"I don't know if we each have a destiny, or if
we're all just floatin' around accidental-like on
a breeze. But I, I think maybe it's both."*

~ FORREST GUMP

"After 9/11/2001, firefighters were honored all over the world. It was 2004, three years later. I had come down to Tampa with my wife to her sister's house for a few days to get away. We were sitting on the patio having breakfast. They had just had the Gasparilla Day Parade– a big event in Florida," remembers Mike Besignano.

Mike's sister-in-law handed him a local newspaper and as he unfolded it, lo and behold, there is Michael Behette on the front page!

"There was Mike on the cover, with beads all around his neck, in uniform, shaking hands with a police officer. Hundreds of firefighters were invited to march; about one hundred were able to attend. I couldn't believe that the one day I was in Florida, and the one newspaper I read, there was Mike Behette on the front page!" exclaims Besigano. "That's not the end of the story, he continued. "Two years later, we moved to Florida. I have the Tampa Tribune delivered. It was the weekend of September 11th. On Sundays, they play football. Apparently, Mike Alstott, who played for the Buccaneers, invited FDNY members to run onto the field in honor of the brothers. I got a phone call from my friend Dave King asking if I could make, but I couldn't. I was with my folks about 100 miles away. I couldn't make it.

"The next day, I'm back home. I get my newspaper out of my driveway. I sit down, unfold the newspaper, and there on the first page is Michael Behette, strutting on the field, all by himself, right on the front page! They had about a hundred guys and they all ran out with American flags, but not Mike. He got to carry the Bucs' Flag!

"I call him up, 'Hey Mike, you did it again!' 'What are you talking about?' he said. He had no idea.

"Always in the right place at the right time, almost like Forrest Gump– so quiet, soft spoken. I guess it was also his looks. Everyone likes to see a handsome New York City fireman on the cover of the news. Only Mike could make the cover of an out-of-town newspaper, not once, but twice!" said Mike Besignano.

On September 9, 2006, reporter Martin Fennelly shared the following news in The Tampa Tribune (Florida): Real Heroes to Lead Out Bucs for Opener:

Instead of seeing football players running from the tunnel at Raymond James Stadium to open their season, the world will see members of the Fire Department of the City of New York. These were the men that five years earlier had stood atop the remains of the World Trade Center. The Pile. After doing those arduous jobs, they went back to 'Work.'

"They're the heroes. If you ask the heroes (about it), they hand you a beer and say enough with the hero stuff. It's what they do." Mike Alstott, former American football player with the Tampa Bay Buccaneers said.

It was Dave Pacheco, a firefighter in Truck Co. 53 in Safety Harbor, who approached the Bucs about tickets for the guys for Sunday's opener with Baltimore. Mike Alstott loves firefighters. Same goes for teammate Dave Moore, who's from New Jersey and who lost friends on 9/11.

Alstott came up with tickets for Dave Pacheco's guys. Then came the idea: Why not have the guys lead the Bucs out?

Pacheco, who goes by Chico, loved the idea because he loves the guys from New York.

He met them five years ago. Like a lot of firefighters around the country, Pacheco went to New York after 9/11. He worked at the Trade Center. He went to funerals. He became friends with the FDNY guys. Friends they remain. That's how a brotherhood works.

DANCING
~ JOHN SOREZZA REMEMBERS

"... I may be totally wrong but I'm a Dancing Fool ..."

~FRANK ZAPPA, DANCIN' FOOL

As a teenager, Mike enjoyed hanging out at a tiny club on Third Avenue called *Jasmine's*, with its mirror-lined interior, or any of the other popular Bay Ridge discos, but as he grew older Mike disliked the idea of dancing clubs... at first. It took his friend John Sorezza quite a bit of time and effort to convince him to try the New Jersey club scene. What he discovered in New Jersey were women closer to his own age and a chance to really let loose.

"I knew Mike from Bay Ridge for about the last 10 years of his life," said John. "I met him through Kevin Boyce. Mike didn't like to do many things all the time but we persuaded him to go to nightclubs with us, and when he did there was no stopping him!

"I was known as City John. A bartender in Manhattan called me that and it stuck forever. Mike's favorite place was *Buona Sera* in Red Bank, New Jersey. Everyone knows that Mike never liked to stay in one place too long, but he enjoyed this place to the point that he never wanted to leave. He actually got up and danced! We went there for about eight years. I would drive there and he would drive home. He never liked to drink; he only had one drink, if any, and he was always the one that had to drive us home.

"Pat Corbett, Mike, and I were all about 6'4" so we really did stand out in the crowds." John continues, "One of the main things that happened during those nights out was that Mike was able to truly enjoy himself and let himself be free. The women there were over 35 years old, so he felt more comfortable among them. He never had any issues with anybody because, basically, he didn't know anybody, so that was good. He met a lot of women and danced to a lot of music from the 70s and 80s. It was a big thing for him. We tried to get there about twice a month. Our trips to *Buona Sera* allowed Mike to have a great time. When he was out dancing, he was relaxed and laid back, with not a care in the world. I can only tell you that we had many good times with the women we met, but I can't get into any more details because we have to keep it PG. It may not be a lot of information but it is all good information."

In 2001, John was a part of a group of over 60 friends that went to New Orleans to see the Jets play the Saints. "After the game, a fight broke out in the streets," remembers John. "What could've been ugly turned friendly when some of the guys announced they were firefighters from New York and the crowds started cheering for them. It was good to get that kind of support from the rest of the country."

SUCH A NICE BOY
~ PHILOMENA CAPODANNO REMEMBERS

"Mike was with my family during a trip to Lourdes," remembers Philomena, Michael's friend Raymond's 94 year-old mother. "It was a very emotional experience for all of us. We had some very nice experiences and actually met a young lady from the States who was staying with her aunt and working in Lourdes as a volunteer, helping the sick people. I thought she and Michael looked kind of cute together. He was shocked to find out that her mother was close to his age. She looked quite mature and Michael had such a beautiful boyish face, they were both fooled.

"Anyway, behind the cathedral in Lourdes, France, is a hill where a trail has been cut and the Stations of the Cross have been installed. Each station consists of an event in the Passion of Christ and is memorialized with life-sized statues of all the participants. This is a very moving journey. The young lady took us on a personal tour. I think she had a crush on Michael, although he wasn't interested in her like that.

"In the evening, in spite of the vast amount of restaurants in the vicinity, most of them were closed. But once you pass through the gates of the Sanctuary, peace and tranquility surround you, so we wanted to stay. Even amid thousands of pilgrims, you can experience quiet and tranquility. We decided that we would sit on the floor and have a picnic. My son Raymond went out and found a deli that was open and a pizzeria. He bought cold cuts and breads and other things to eat and the young lady, my husband, Raymond, Michael, and I enjoyed our dinner picnic on the grounds of Lourdes.

Our next stop on the train was Spain. The ride was twelve hours, and the train had quite a few young children on it. Needless to say, they began to get restless. Little by little, Michael had everyone's attention; even the ones who didn't speak English were glued to this gentle giant of a man. He had the kids in the corner where there was a little space and he entertained them with his antics and a few tricks. It was like watching the Pied Piper. Before we stopped in Spain, Michael went to the food car while the children anxiously waited for him. When he returned, he had ice cream for everyone, including himself!

"On the plane ride back to the States, Michael gave me a gift from Lourdes, even though we were there together. He handed me a bag with a beautiful gold-framed picture of the Blessed Mother; I still have it. It is just as beautiful today as it was the day he presented it to me.

"While we were in France, where my family lives, Michael had a chance to meet and visit with my niece Michelle and her family. He never forgot her hospitality and her pizzas and paella. When Michelle came to visit in 2004, first he picked them up at the airport, without us asking him to. When he found out Raymond was working, he volunteered. Before we made any plans, Mike purchased tickets to a New York Knicks game in Madison Square Garden. He had ringside seats and bought the kids American hotdogs, sodas, and little trinkets to have fun with at the game. He wanted her and the three kids to have a real American experience, and they did! Who could forget a night like that?

My husband and I have wonderful memories of Michael and his beautiful smile. Whenever he saw us in Brooklyn, walking home from shopping on 86th Street, he would pull over and stop the car, take our packages, and made sure to drive us home. That's the kind of boy he was.

When we visited Michael in the hospital, he had been quite weakened and sleepy. I sat next to him with his mother, a dear woman. I told her how much we loved Michael and that he was more than just Raymond's dear friend, he was family to us. She was amazed at how many endearing stories she heard about her wonderful son. Sometimes a mother needs to hear these things.

When he stirred about, I spoke to him, 'Michael, this is Mrs. Capodanno, and I'm here to see you, dear.' I saw his eyes pop open and as weak as he was, he took my hand and gave it a kiss. How could I ever forget such a thing? Never!

I feel so bad losing such a wonderful boy but I know that he is in heaven and we will all meet again one day. He is smiling down on us," said Philomena.

Supporting a Dream
- *Jennifer Hayek Remembers*

> *"Fame. I'm gonna live forever. I'm gonna learn how to fly high. I feel it coming together. People will see me and cry. Fame!*
>
> ~Songwriters: John Lennon, David Bowie, Carlos Alomar

Jennifer Hayek is Mike's cousin from Ohio with whom he had a special connection. She has fond memories of watching the Tony Awards and the Academy Awards shows with Mike – albeit from different states!

Mike supported her acting career and always gave her encouragement. "I'm watching your career. I want a full report," he'd tease her. He was more of a big brother than a cousin to Jennifer. Even if they didn't see each other or speak often, he was always checking up on her. "How's life treating you? You okay? How's it going with the theater?" He was genuinely interested in her career.

"When I lived in Manhattan for a few years, Mike would meet up with me for a drink," Jennifer remembers. "Whenever we went, with other cousins or friends, Mike always wanted to show us something new. Something he discovered and wanted to share with us. If we went on top of a building to have a drink on a rooftop, he would say, 'You see?

I know how to get into everywhere.' Once we went into a bar in Bryant Park. I saw things I would never see in Ohio!"

For his Ohio cousin, a trip to Bay Ridge's *Wicked Monk* was an adventure. Mike knew all the local hangouts in Bay Ridge – *Skinflints, The Salty Dog, Kettle Blacks, Bennet's, Greenhouse Café*, to name a few – and he enjoyed taking Jennifer along with their Canadian cousin, Dedie. That was his thing. In a quiet way, he always tried to make everyone feel very special, and he did. He was known and welcomed in all the establishments. The irony was that he didn't even drink! Even sipping his cranberry cocktails for hours, he was always a welcomed guest.

Since Mike loved to travel, Jennifer would ask him to visit Ohio. "Ohio! What's in Ohio?" he would respond. "Nah, I'm alright."

Jennifer had been performing in Ohio for over 20 years and her dream was to come to New York City. Her dream became a reality when she attended the *American Academy of Dramatic Arts School* on Madison Avenue to study theater and film. When she graduated, Michael was right there alongside her mother at the ceremony.

Mike was also right there to support her when it came time for her very first performance. Jennifer recalls, "I invited a bunch of people, but only Mikey was able to come. There he stood in the audience, all by himself – literally. He was the only person that showed up! It was a Thursday night and the theater was completely empty except for Mike. The director knew he was my cousin and the only live member of the audience. He was debating whether to go on with the show or just call it a night. Mike got so agitated, he told him, 'Come on! Just do the show! I'm already here, just *do* it already!'

"So we did it – all 3 ½ hours of William Shakespeare! He was so annoyed the whole time. We couldn't help looking at him. He was rolling his eyes and checking his phone. When it was over – 3 ½ hours later – I asked him, 'What did you think?' 'I *hated* it,' he said, 'Come on. Let's get a drink.' What a trooper! The poor guy looked like he was in pain! The after show was so much better than the show! We had a drink and he dropped me off at my apartment and went home. The rest of the crew stayed behind. Mikey didn't want anything to do with that performance anymore. He always said that if he were to act, he'd have to start at the top!"

Another Fifteen Minutes of Fame – *Joe LiVolsi remembers*

"The nice thing about being a celebrity is that, if you bore people, they think it's their fault."

~Henry A. Kissinger

"I will always admire Mike for his unselfishness, his generosity, his strength, and his courage. I will also never forget his ability to get his face on TV and meet famous people, like the time at the Concert for New York City after 9/11. He calls me and tells me that he got backstage and met Paul McCartney, Billy Joel, Robert De Niro, Mick Jagger, and many others.

"So, I come home from work and put on the Yankees playoff game. I start telling my wife about all the people Mike met, and as I look at the TV, I yell, 'There he is!'

"Sure enough, the camera zooms in on Mike standing behind a big American flag. Classic Mike.

I love you, Mike. God bless you."

Smokin' Joe LiVolsi

The Thanksgiving Parade
~ *Jennifer Hayek remembers*

*"But Thanksgiving is more than eating, Chuck.
You heard what Linus was saying out there. Those
pilgrims were thankful for what had happened to
them, and we should be thankful, too. We should just
be thankful for being together. I think that's what
they mean by 'Thanksgiving,' Charlie Brown."*

~MARCIE, *A CHARLIE BROWN THANKSGIVING*

About ten years before Michael passed, his Ohio cousin Jennifer Hayek recalls a wonderful Thanksgiving reunion. As is true for so many Americans, Thanksgiving is a time to get together with family. In Michael's case, that included the Canadian family, the Ohio family, and of course, the Brooklyn side of the clan.

This particular year the weather was very cold as Mike took Jennifer, Giselle, and Yolanda to the *Macy's Annual Thanksgiving Day Parade* in Manhattan. "We were freezing!" Jennifer recalls. "He didn't care. All he kept talking about was the fact that he could get right to the front of the line, right to the top. And we did. But the girls couldn't stop complaining about the freezing cold. Finally, to shut us up, he disappeared for a while and when he returned, he handed each of us a piping hot cup of hot chocolate to keep us warm and quiet. Before long, we were up at the front where the parade actually began, watching all the players warm up before the festivities. Handlers were already struggling to hold onto the giant character balloons."

"As the girls drank their cocoa, Mike made it his business to schmooze and mingle with all the firefighters and law enforcers positioned along the floats, ready to keep the peace and the festivities in order. He just talked to everybody, even if he never met them before. He had a way of making everyone feel comfortable, like he knew you for a hundred years. There were hugs and high-fives all over. The girls and I just followed behind him. We had to keep up and keep moving because Mikey would get restless if we were in one spot for too long. So, like the parade, we just kept marching through!" Jennifer recalls. "What made Michael love the parade? Perhaps it was the ever-changing line-ups every year, the performers, the floats, The *Radio City Rockettes*, or Santa Claus closing up the Parade and kicking off the holidays in NYC. All I know is that it wasn't the only parade Michael loved, and what he enjoyed more than the parade was sharing it with friends and loved ones. It was through his joy that the Parade became even more special to those around him."

And the Winner Is...
- Dawn Bergen remembers

"Every great film should seem new every time you see it."

~Roger Ebert

Mike had an enthusiasm for awards shows, along with a knack for picking Academy Awards winners. So it was no surprise when he met Dawn Bergen at a wedding, that they would hit it off because of her equal passion. Dawn remembers being introduced to Mike and learning all about him in a very short period, even though she was with a different group of people. They seemed to click and he ended the night saying, "I'm going to call you. Alright? I'm going to call you." If he said it once, he said it a hundred times. And call her he did.

They went to one of Mike's favorite theaters, the *Angelika Film Center & Café* on Houston Street in Manhattan. He had spent many hours there since it's opening in 1989, enjoying independent, foreign, or obscure indie films and documentaries. The thing about Mike was, if he wanted to see a film, he went, even if it was alone. This time though, Mike and Dawn saw a movie that turned out to be one of Mike's all-time favorites, *Slumdog Millionaire*. At the Academy Awards, *Slumdog Millionaire* won eight of the ten awards for which it was nominated. Mike told everyone to go see it.

Dawn remembers, "I knew Michael two years before he was diagnosed with cancer. We shared a passion for movies and Broadway shows. Mike was sure to check out all the shows that were nominated so that he could formulate an educated opinion about them before awards night."

Besides sharing his enthusiasm for theater and film, he gave Dawn and her mother a wonderful memory to cherish the rest of their lives.

"Hey. It's me, Mike," the conversation began. "Do you have a fancy dress for tonight?" Still not knowing the occasion, Dawn couldn't imagine where she was going. "We're going to see the Tony Awards tonight. And we're going to take your mother, too."

"First, I was shocked to even find out that we could actually go to see the Tonys. I thought only movie stars went," said Dawn. "When I told him, he just made it seem like the most natural thing in the world. 'Nah, nah, regular people go,' he said. 'You just have to get dressed up. They prefer that you wear black tuxedoes. If you get filmed, you have to blend in.'

"He had to make a run to Kohl's to get a new bowtie and cummerbund because he had lent his out to someone and never got it back. When he was all dressed up, he kept asking me, 'How do I look? How do I look?'" Dawn remembers, "He looked great. Fit right in with the movie stars!

"Just like that, Mike, my mom, and I were at the *63rd Annual Tony Awards* at *Radio City Music Hall* in New York City! Neil Patrick Harris was the host. Not only did Mike look great and handsome, he knew his shows and he knew all of the insider tips.

"The show was nonstop entertainment, starting with the themes of every Broadway show," said Dawn. "If you ever have an opportunity, pull a 'Mike' and go on *Craig's List* for tickets to the Tony Awards.

"Mike loved his foreign films and *Slumdog* was definitely one of his favorites. You know Mike," Dawn added, "If he loved something, it was the best! And nobody could tell him otherwise!"

Mike had a determination when it came to entertainment. It meant nothing to him if a show or an event was sold out. He would leave his friends or date on a line, saying, "Stay there," and then return with freshly-scalped tickets. He knew the scalpers and he even had his favorites. "In 2012, a group of us went to see *Porgy and Bess*," Dawn recalls, "It was probably the last time we went to see a play together."

(Top Left) Susan Olsson, Mimi Kamouh,
and Mike in New Orleans, 2001 (Top Right) Mike with
Dawn Bergen at The Tony Awards (Middle) Sam Grillo, Mike,
Jimmy Herro, Denise Grillo (Middle Right and Bottom)
Jet Games with good friends

Seeing the Ball Drop
- *John Olsson, Jr. remembers*

"… I'm walking down Times Square
in the electric daylight…"

~ *Elvis Costello*

" Mike and my parents had been friends since before I was born. I always remember him being around my house and being a part of our lives," recalls John Olsson, Jr. "One New Year's Eve, I was seeing a girl, and she really wanted to go to Times Square. When Mike heard about her request, he wasted no time in setting us up. That night, we met outside the barriers. He was already retired, but in no time we were able to get through four checkpoints. It meant so much to him to make everything work out just right for us. He used all his pull to get us right up there between the stage and the ball. I felt sorry for all those people who were waiting for hours in the cold. We got there at 11 p.m. and by 11:45, we were at the ball! After the ball dropped, we made our way back to 8th Avenue and met up with him again. He gave us a ride back home to Staten Island, even though he lived in Brooklyn. There aren't many people that would do all that for you, but he did it with all his heart.

"Mike also gave me advice about women– something about having 'a girl in every port,' continued John. "I do remember him bringing a different girl to every one of my birthday parties, and he did come to every party!"

John always admired Mike and how he selflessly made his way back from Florida on 9/11 to be among his brothers and fellow New Yorkers. He recalled that even when he became sick, his body deteriorated, but his personality only grew stronger. It shined until the very end. "Mike always dropped by a party or for a visit, even if it was only for half an hour. We used to call it an 'Irish exit'—leaving without saying goodbye. But with Mike, no one really ever got mad because Mike always came to be with you.

"What he did professionally was a direct reflection of his personality. Even as a kid, I knew he was special. Being a fireman and running into a fire isn't what most people would do. He was definitely a good role model to me," said John.

WHERE EVERYBODY KNOWS YOUR NAME...
~ *EDDIE MORGAN REMEMBERS*

Growing up in Bay Ridge, going to the bars and clubs was considered a rite of passage. As the years go by, some faces may fade but others will always shine. Even though Mike was not a heavy drinker–most times he didn't drink at all – he attended the local watering holes often to visit with a friend or sit with the bartenders and waiters. He made friends wherever he went, and he was often remembered for his extraordinary personality.

Eddie Morgan (aka Mike's Favorite Bartender) fondly remembers this anecdote: "Mike is one of the best guys I ever knew. He had a heart of gold. Family and friends always came first, especially his FDNY family. I remember one night in *Lyons Bar*, I asked him, 'Why are you still working all of these holiday shifts? You've been on the job a long time now.' His reply was, 'I cover for the guys who have kids at home!'"

An Interview on the Scene with Larry King

Television and radio host Brooklyn-born Larry King visited *Ground Zero* within a few weeks of the buildings' collapse to witness the scene first-hand and to speak with the rescue workers. Using his signature no-nonsense, hands-on approach, he spoke to Thomas Von Essen, who was Fire Commissioner at the time. Among the firefighters interviewed in the segment, which can be seen on YouTube *(see: 9/11 Larry King At Ground Zero CNN Special Oct 6 2001)*, was Michael Babette. The Commissioner explained to Larry King that at first, rescue and recovery crews refused to give up hope that they would pull someone alive from the wreckage, but that he could sense that the mood was shifting from a hopeful excitement to a more somber attitude as they realized that wasn't likely to happen. Still, recovering bodies was viewed as an important task– one that would give their fallen comrades some dignity in death.

Pausing his intense labor on *The Pile*, Mike and his partner went over to greet Larry King. The conversation, which has received Larry King's permission to quote, went something like this:

"Hi. How are ya? I see your show all the time. Nice to meet you," says Michael Behette as he approaches. With a hearty handshake that conveyed respect and gratitude, Larry greeted both firefighters. Mike introduced his partner as Ladder 247 and himself as 173. The surprise of seeing a celebrity suddenly faded as Mike remembered why he was there and plunged into an explanation of what was going on at that moment. Standing among

the 110 stories that had been reduced to 80 feet of rubble, the informal interview began. The world was watching via the non-stop media coverage, but only few understood exactly what the rescue and recovery workers were bearing every day.

King spoke to the men, inquiring about their roles. "We go through the rubble. When they find a body; we put him in a bag and bring it out," Mike informs him.

"Are you finding something every day?" Larry asks.

"Some days we don't find anything. Other days we find groups of guys. It varies from day to day...so much rubble," his partner answers.

"How do you ever get used to that?" Larry wants to know.

"We just do it. I've been here every other day since the attacks. The destruction is unbelievable. There are still over 5,000 bodies; we haven't found everyone," Mike adds. (At the time, it was estimated that over 6,000 victims may have been buried beneath the wreckage.)

"And you can still smell it?" Larry asks.

"You can smell it," Mike says as he reaches into the upper pouch of his tan overalls, to pull out a small cobalt blue bottle of over-the-counter Vicks Vapor Rub. The same product that mothers rubbed onto babies' chests to bring them warm, comforting relief at bedtime from sniffles and congestion. "They give us this, to take away from the stench."

Then Michael pulls up the air-filtering respirator mask, showing Larry King what was supposed to be the ultimate protection. "They give us this, too. This is for the asbestos and dust. So, we're pretty well ...." He hesitates to finish the sentence with the word "protected" because as a firefighter, perhaps he knew the truth– that he was never fully protected.

"No way you could've trained for this?" Larry asks the two men.

"Ah, man, no way," replies Michael.

"It's beyond all training. It's an act of war," the Firefighter from Ladder 247 replies.

"How many hours are you working?" Larry wants to know.

"I've been working here every other day, 13-hour shifts. The schedule is overwhelming. On Sunday, we went to two funerals– Dave Weiss, who

we used to work with at Ladder 172*. Then there was Chief Palmer. Then Monday I had to work, Tuesday I had to work, Wednesday we're here. Tomorrow we have another funeral that I have to go Upstate to, then tomorrow night I have to go back to work and Friday I have to work. It seems to be all we do is work and go to funerals," Mike concluded.

* David Martin Weiss was a firefighter with the Elite Rescue Company 1, who was appointed to the FDNY in November of 1989 after being awarded Emily Trevor-Mary B. Warren Medal for Heroism. In 1997, he rescued a man whose car had plunged into the East River from the FDR Drive. Weiss was off-duty when he witnessed the accident, climbed over the road barrier and jumped into the river to rescue the driver, whose heart had given out.

Firefighter Weiss succumbed to injuries sustained while operating at Manhattan 5th Alarm Box at 2 World Trade Center on September 11, 2001.

Nearly 3,000 people died in the terror attack that day, the worst-ever attack on US soil. The body count was shocking, and the suffering by victims' families hard to reflect. However, the repercussions are far from over. The 'shadow victims' – people who inhaled the toxic dust cloud that enveloped Ground Zero – include shopkeepers, office workers, local residents, students, first responders, emergency service, and volunteers who were exposed to the site at close quarters. These victims are now suffering serious, and in some cases fatal, illnesses as a direct result. Indeed, far more people are likely to die from the effects of the dust than in the attack itself.

In the end, it was realized that *Ground Zero* was about the most dangerous workplace imaginable. The smoking heap of nearly two million tons of tangled steel and concrete contained a witches' brew of toxins, asbestos, benzene PCB's, and hundreds of chemicals. People are now paying with their lives. Besides dealing with the aftermath of a terrorist attack, some say it has turned into a full blown environmental attack on the scale of Chernobyl, where the initial toll was overshadowed by the deaths and illnesses that were occurring up to 20 years later.

These victims, like Michael, have had to go to extraordinary lengths to be seen or heard or treated; their stories deserve to be more widely told.

The Long and Winding Road.... to Gasparilla

Five months after 9/11, Mike was among the many workers who were at Ground Zero for long shifts, working overtime digging through the rubble. Time off was spent comforting friends, widows, and children. They had no time for rest, barely any time for their own families.

It was Firefighter Brian Muldowney from the Hillsborough County Fire Station in Tampa, Florida who realized that those guys needed a break, and did something about it.

Brian had spent eight long weeks at the sight looking for his own brother Richie Muldowney, who was a member of Ladder 7 in Manhattan. On September 11th, Richie was supposed to get off at 9 a.m. His relief hadn't showed up by the time the first plane hit, so he hopped on his Ladder 7 and headed off.

Richie was a blue-eyed, robust Irishman with a red handlebar mustache and a hearty laugh. He was a great cook and his meals were always appreciated by the firefighters. He was the goalie on the firehouse hockey team. Much like Mike, during his bachelor days, he was always willing to work overtime so the others could spend time with their families. Once he married, he was a devoted family man.

It was Brian's admiration for his brother that inspired him to become a firefighter. Like Mike, Brian and Richie had a history of cops and firefighters in their family.

Back in Tampa, despite his own grief, Brian recognized that the FDNY men needed a little break and a little commendation. At the fire station, he shared his idea to bring the men down to Tampa to lead the

Gasparilla Parade, and it didn't take long for the whole community to rally and made it happen, complete with a hero's welcome in Tampa. For many across the country, it was a relief to learn that not all firefighters and rescue workers had perished in the 9/11 attacks and rescue efforts.

In February 2002, the city of Tampa was ready for the annual celebration commemorating the exploits of Pirate José Gasper, the pirate believed to have roamed the Caribbean in the early 19th century with his outlaw crew. Nearly every year for the past century, a mock pirate attack is staged in the city of Tampa. Floats resembling fully-rigged pirate ships with masked and elaborately costumed participants "float" down the streets to festive music. The parade attracts over 300,000 spectators and that day, men, women, and children crowded the FDNY float. There were exchanges of brightly colored beads sporting mermaids and lobsters, coins, garter belts, and more as the appreciative crowds shouted "We love you!" and begged for the simple black disc that simply said "FDNY."

The FDNY were stationed on the third float, behind The Tampa Bay Firefighters' Krewe Of Saint Florian and in front of the Lido marching band. The Krewe of Saint Florian (the patron saint of firefighters) was composed of career firefighters from the Tampa Bay area. How uplifting it was for the FDNY to be among such brothers!

By the time they passed the Tampa Convention Center, the firefighters had ran out of the 20,000 strands of black discs, but the cheers and good wishes and shouts of "We love you guys!" remained strong.

Mike Behette probably slapped about 500 hands that day. Dressed in his Class A dress uniform, navy pants, a light blue shirt and a navy jacket, with a patch sewn into the left sleeve. "It's 35 degrees and pouring in New York City," Michael said, as the Tampa heat and the heaviness of his uniform caused him to sweat. "This sure takes us away." For Mike, like the others it was good to wear the uniform again for something good and fun. They all had seen too many memorial services.

"Wave to the heroes," Mike heard parents tell their children at the parade that day. "It's all so great, but it's sort of bittersweet, you know?" Mike said. "It's hard not to think about why we're here." He knew that even though the memorials were coming to a close, firefighters continued to search for friends lost and struggled to find a way to deal with their grief.

Heroes' day in the sun

Firefighters shed New York gloom for warm Gasparilla welcome

FHP Trooper L.M. Inge, left, shakes hands with firefighter Mike Beherte of Ladder Company 172 in Brooklyn during Saturday's Gasparilla parade in Tampa.

"Blessed are the pure of heart, for they shall see God." ~ *A mother remembers*

"All the fruits of Michael's actions point to Michael seeing God in everyone he meets.

My son Michael entered the New York City Fire Department on September 5, 1981. He neither sought high positions, nor accepted any recognition for the many heroic endeavors he made. 'It's all a part of my job,' he would say.

"His professional and personal demeanors are one and the same. When needed, whether by strangers, friends or family, Michael just helped. No questions asked. He was the glue that kept a large circle of friends together. Jobless? He found them work. Downtrodden? He encouraged them. Hurting? He listened. Sick? He handed them Rosary Beads, usually from Lourdes, and when someone like Yolanda Gonzales' parents needed transportation to medical facilities, he drove them and patiently waited– all day if necessary– for them to finish doctor appointments. His patience was boundless when it came to others. He simply gave and always from his heart. His most common words were 'Whatever you want, I am a phone call away.'

"Michael's joy was to see everyone around him happy. He always gave his best to make sure they were. Michael was a pure and kindred spirit to so many people."

He had the Moves
~ Clare Mazza remembers

"Every savage can dance."

~Jane Austen, Pride and Prejudice

"I met Michael back in the 1970s during the disco era. He was introduced to me as "Bubbles" and the name just stuck. – not sure if he liked it. I do remember he called me his best "pal," said Clare.

Saturday Night Fever put Bay Ridge on the national map. Of course, the places from the movies are mostly gone, such as the *2001 Odyssey Club* on 64th Street. At least the Verrazano Bridge connecting Brooklyn to Staten Island, and loomed largely in the movie, still remains. When the movie was made in 1974, the bridge had only opened a little more than a decade earlier. Another thing that remains the same is the house where Tony Manero lived in with his parents, sister, and grandmother. It was located at 221 79th street.

Back in the 1970s and through the 1980s, Michael and Clare and other friends often went dancing together. There was something about that disco rhythm that got your feet and body moving. It was a time of glimmering disco balls, the Hustle, and the Bee Gees playing *Staying Alive*.

"Michael had his own dance moves. He planted his feet firmly on the ground and just moved his body around. It was a unique move for the time and he looked great doing it. He insisted that it was the only way to dance and said I should practice the moves," remembers Clare.

Even when the music wasn't full-on disco, people still got up and danced. Queen's *Another One Bites the Dust* had a good beat and the music was danceable. The disco crowds went crazy and Mike stuck to his dance moves. There were plenty of places to shine in Bay Ridge such as *Jasmine's*, *Revelations*, *Penthouse* and when those became passé, there were the Long Island joints, such as *Speakeasy*.

"Several years ago it came in handy. I was at a wedding but my leg was hurting and I probably shouldn't have attempted to dance. I remembered how he stood in one spot with his feet planted on the ground, and how he allowed his giant body to gyrate to the music. I gave it a try! I loved to dance. Sure enough it worked! I was able to dance "Bubbles' Dance, as I dubbed it.

"It was great and I even received a few compliments. I knew he would be happy to think he taught me how to dance," recalls Clare.

"On October 2, 2011, amongst the dancing and eating the streets, I spent the day with Michael, Giselle and my best friend, Barbara, at the Third Avenue Feast in Brooklyn," says Clare.

The 38th annual Third Avenue Festival consisted of 27 blocks along the Ridge's lowest-numbered commercial strip celebrating all day long with food, music, dancing and fun. About 200,000 people showed up for the party.

The Feast gave visitors and locals a chance to check out the many local restaurants, their diverse ethnic foods, and lots of live dancing on the streets.

Restaurant owners on the Avenue set up sidewalk cafés for you to sit back and relax. We stopped at *the Green House Café*, sat at a table and chatted.

"In 2012, Barbara and I spent some time with Michael's brother, Tony, and his family at the same Third Avenue Feast," says Clare.

The festival route was full of concert stages, where singers and dancers entertained the crowds all day long. Vendors along the festival route sold all sorts of treats, like cotton candy, crepes, corn on the cob, sausage sandwiches, and more. There were lots of carnival games and rides, including pony rides for children.

"It was good to spend two years in a row with the Behette family. The only thing missing was Michael.

"I constantly pray for Michael and will always remember the quality time Michael, Barbara and I spent together. Just three old friends cherishing what we had with each other. He'll always hold a special place in my heart," remembers Clare.

The Brooklyn/Florida Connection
~ Michael Benson remembers

*"We didn't start the fire. It was always burning since
the world's been turning. We didn't start the fire.
No, we didn't light it, but we tried to fight it…"*

~ Billy Joel

With a population of approximately 2.5 million people of every ethnicity, there is always something happening in Brooklyn. Whatever could happen in the city that never sleeps, eventually happens in Brooklyn.

Mike had a million stories about things that happened on the job and he never missed an opportunity to share one. Furthermore, if he could, he would involve you right in one. He often spoke of the adrenaline rush he felt plowing through walls, or the excitement that pulsed throughout his veins leaping from fire escape to fire escape. He knew that every fire was unique, and that he needed all his senses to fight this very dangerous devil. As unnerving as it is, it becomes a firefighter's duty to forge on until it is conquered. It is a matter of life and death and the responsibility weighs heavy on every firefighter's shoulders. The devoutness to their service pushes them forward even when human nature tells them just the opposite. Perhaps sharing that unspoken creed of devotion is what binds firefighters to each other. Mike was no different; he couldn't do enough to help his fellow firefighters. When the opportunity presented itself to help an old friend's son– a newbie firefighter– naturally Mike was "all in."

Sometimes people are born into friendships – they become inter-generational. For Michael Benson, it was his grandparents who origi-nally knew the Behette family. Michael Behette visited the Benson family with his mother, Madeleine, when he was a child and would of-ten sit with the senior Mr. Benson, the patriarch of the family and have talks, honing his gift for communicating with people of all ages.

"Even though I came years later, I knew all about Michael's family be-cause of the connection in the 1960s," said Mike Benson. Like Michael Behette, Mike Benson became a firefighter. He joined the Pembroke Pines Fire Department near Fort Lauderdale, Florida. He was new and learning the ropes. He had always heard good things about his family's friends in Brooklyn, the Behettes.

"As a firefighter in South Florida, I thought about what it must be like in New York City, one of the busiest fire departments in the na-tion," remembers Benson. "I know that most people wonder why fire-men are crazy enough to run into burning buildings. They question why we would risk our lives. Well, that question can only be answered by the desire each one of us has to help others, to protect and serve. It is definitely something that is in our blood."

Meanwhile in New York, Michael Behette had found out about the rookie grandson of his old friend, the senior Mr. Benson. Knowing that Mike Benson had joined the brotherhood of firefighters, it only came natural to Behette to reach out and invite him to join him on his next visit back to New York. He was anxious to show him what it was like to be a firefighter in the FDNY.

One day, while visiting his grandmother in Brooklyn, Benson did just that. "I called Michael out of the blue, knowing he was the man to show me the true workings of the FDNY. He promptly responded by making arrangements for me to ride on Engine 88, while he rode Ladder 58. We did the night tour riding from 7 p.m. to 7 a.m."

Michael picked him up and took him to the Firehouse 177 where they got ready for the action or, hopefully non-action that any day as a fire-fighter could bring. "He introduced me as a family cousin and that night we had a few calls– fire alarms, car accidents– I just loved it! As we went along, he showed me all the ropes and inside operations of the FDNY," Mike remembers.

He rode the fire truck with fierceness and velocity, with the adrena-line pumping and ready to spring into action no matter how big or small the job was. It was clear Michael was in his element when duty called. The next morning, he took Mike home.

Two days later a big fire went down. Half the block was burned to the ground. "When it was over, Mike was still pumped with adrenaline," remembers Benson. "I think if he could've picked me up on the way to the fire, he would have. It's tough to come down when everything is up– the stress level, the heart rate, and pulse rate. Even blood pressure rises during these circumstances."

It was his day off, but Mike went back to the site to show Benson what had gone down. "The fire was out, but men were still there cleaning up. They were overhauling, going through the building, making sure there weren't any more hotspots in the carpets or the walls or on a couch or bed. You have to go in and clean, it's re-ally messy work. Although we were itching, we weren't allowed to do anything because of liability, so we stood across the street, took some pictures and then later met up with the guys," Benson remem-bers. "Getting to know Michael in those days was an experience I will never forget. He hardly knew me, but our family connection was so strong he accepted me right away. He was genuine and caring. I'll always appreciate that he took time out of his busy life and gave me such great memories.

"Michael was also very funny. I had a great time with the guys in the firehouse. They had such high energy and that great New York accent, and it was just fun listening to the guys say, 'Hayyy, Bahettttte!'"

After 9/11, Benson came to New York City again with a group from his church. He didn't get to see Mike during that visit because he was too busy working at *The Pile*.

"We talked on the phone a bit, but he would never leave *The Pile*," Benson remembers. Benson and members from his church were in the area serving meals and visiting the various firehouses, talking to the guys, trying to keep morale up. "It was terrible, everyone was grieving and stressed, but they opened their hearts and were loving to us. We had no schedules—just chitchatted, had meals, rode on the truck. We related to them, not as tragically, but as brothers. All firefighters have their share of sadness and difficult times," he recalls.

"In the last years, Michael and my own dad developed a connection in their relationship. They both had been very sick and, as Christians, they bonded and gave encouragement to each other," says Benson. Though they each suffered with cancer, they were able to offer each other spiritual and moral support through a visit and phone calls. "When my dad was near the end, I remember finding a photo of Michael standing in front of the trucks. It was from that memorable day in Brooklyn. I gave my dad the picture; he kept it on his nightstand. I believe they gave each other some comfort.

"My experiences with Michael were short, but my memories of him and the experiences we had will last my lifetime. He welcomed me like family, went above and beyond to allow me to experience the FDNY. But it was not just about the FDNY– Michael Behette taught me what it meant to be a truly loving, giving, and genuine man. Mike was a memorable guy, always respectful of my grandmother. He was funny, graceful, always thinking of others. What a great demeanor! No doubt about it, he loved his job!" remarked Benson.

Brooklyn Neighbors ~ Sheila Benson (from Fort Lauderdale) remembers

We were neighbors with the Behette's for many years and my mother and Madeline were good friends. They were very comfortable in each other's' houses as many neighbors were in the 1960s neighborhoods of Brooklyn, New York. When we moved away, I always asked my mother about the Behette family. All of their children were very nice, respectful.

"We were deeply saddened when we learned Michael was ill. My own husband had developed pancreatic cancer. In 2011, we went to New York for a visit. Michael and my husband were very drawn to each other; they got to talking and discussing their problems in a very spiritual way.

"When we were back in Florida, one day while I was not at home, my husband had an urge to call him. We usually made the phone calls together. He found and called the number on the paper that reached him in the hospital. Madeleine was sitting next to her son as she diligently did, day and night. Too weak to hold the phone himself, his mother put the receiver to his ear. My husband spoke to him through his own tears. He recited *Psalm 23*. A few hours later, Michael had passed away. He was glad that he did not wait for me to make that phone call.

"My husband passed less than three months later. I believe if we are here, God has a purpose for us. He's always in control; we do our best, we pray for guidance.

Psalm 23 - A Psalm of David.
The LORD is my shepherd; there is nothing I lack.
In green pastures, he makes me lie down;
To still waters he leads me; he restores my soul.
He guides me along right paths for the sake of his name.
Even though I walk through the valley of the shadow of death,
I will fear no evil, for you are with me.
Your rod and your staff comfort me.
You set a table before me in front of my enemies.
You anoint my head with oil; my cup overflows.
Indeed, goodness and mercy will pursue me all the days of my life.
I will dwell in the house of the LORD for endless days.

Take the Last Train to Clarksville… Yolanda Garcia Was There

In March of 2002, as part of the *Cities Unite America and Thank New York Firefighters*, two hundred New York City firefighters, selected via lottery, visited two hundred U.S. cities as guests of the mayors in a national effort to thank the firefighters and promote travel and tourism. Michael was encouraged to put his name into the hat for this "traveling ambassador" initiative, which included events such as school visits, parades, luncheons, and street-naming ceremonies. Of course, Michael (along with another firefighter) was selected to be one of the participants!

The two firefighters and their partners were sent off to Clarksville, Tennessee. From the moment they stepped foot on the ground, the red carpet was rolled out for the foursome. Greeted by a fire engine-red limousine and a local firefighter who acted as their tour guide, the town opened their arms and hearts to the group.

The first stop was a local radio station, where the two firemen were interviewed. Next was a bowling event for the 4H Club for children. "We really had no idea what to expect," recalls Yolanda, who accompanied him. "It was just so much fun being their guests and driving around in the fire engine-red limousine. That night, we went to 'The Poor Man's Country Club' for dinner.

"In the mornings, they left us alone for breakfast at our hotel, but everything in the town was gratis for us. The next day, we headed out to Nashville, Tennessee. On the way, we ate at a terrific steakhouse. They claimed it was one of the top ten in the country, and it sure seemed like it to us!

"In Nashville, we were expected at the Grand Ole Opry. It was amazing! They claim that's where the real show is. We got to watch the inner workings of the show and the Opry staffers and artists getting ready for their performances. They gave Michael a book, a sort of Family Album book that people normally purchase, and then have all the performers sign. In anticipation of us coming, they'd had the performers sign over the last month, including Dolly Parton. In addition, all the performers that night wanted to sign. There were stars and superstars and legends of country music. The Opry had about eight or more artist on each show. We couldn't believe it! We were backstage, by invitation and performers were coming to us," remembers Yolanda.

"We were truly humbled. They asked Mike and the other fire fighter to speak to the audience. Michael was not prepared and hesitated. 'Do it, Michael. They really want to meet you,' I said, and he agreed," remembers Yolanda.

"The red curtain rose and with elegance and grace, Michael addressed the crowd. He told them how humbled he was by them having us there. He told them it was he that should be thanking them, not the other way around. He thanked them and the rest of the country for the overwhelming support and loved that had been poured into New York City. No one ever expected it from them, but he was sure glad they did it.

"There weren't many words, but as always with Michael, they came from the heart. He let them know that New York would heal again because of people like them," said Yolanda.

He concluded with 'Thank you very much' and stepped down from the stage. "That wasn't so bad," he whispered to Yolanda.

"To conclude our trip, on the third day, we attended a firefighter picnic where the four of us were the honored guests. They played one of our favorite songs by the Monkees, "*Take the last Train to Clarksville,*" and explained that they had been a little unknown town in Tennessee until the Monkees put them on the map with that song back in August of 1966.

"The two firefighters received special plaques usually reserved for retired firefighters. The wife and I received special plaques as well. We all received t-shirts from the Fire and Police departments and, of course, Mike gave out his t-shirts and caps. They had fire demonstrations to show the children how they fight fires – they demonstrated the equipment. It was a big barbeque on a big property. They also gave the guys axes that were beautifully engraved. The final touch was that each of us received special plaques that said we were honorable citizens of Clarksville, Tennessee. It was quite an honor!" remembers Yolanda.

(Top) Yolanda, Santa and Mike. (Middle Left) Randazzo Christmas Party (Middle Right and Bottom) Clarksville, Tennessee

Never Forgotten Heroes
- *Marianna Randazzo remembers*

*"See, heroes never die. John Wayne isn't dead, Elvis
isn't dead. Otherwise you don't have a hero. You can't
kill a hero. That's why I never let him get older."*

~Mickey Spillane

My name is Marianna Randazzo and this is my Michael Behette story:

In 2004, as a teacher in PS 247 in Brooklyn, I implemented a week of community reading. I invited Mike to read to a group of first graders that I knew would bring the gentle giant to his knees. They did just that as he crawled around the wooden classroom floor to demonstrate a drop and roll procedure. I then invited him to read to the children, something he did not expect, yet did with such love and grace that the children adored him.

"You're tall!' shouted Jessica, a child unafraid to express herself.

"Can I wear your hat?" asked the boy with the red hair and freckles.

Fireman Mike held onto his helmet with a funny, scared look on his face. He was a bit afraid of the little critters. He sat up tall in the very small wooden seat.

"Are you a fireman?" continued the red haired boy.

"Do you go in burning buildings?" asked Joseph. "Is it hot?

These were a few of the questions that my students were shouting at Firefighter Mike as he entered their classroom clutching his helmet close to his body.

Fireman Mike looked a bit confused at first as the 25 children circled around, eyeing him from head to toe, but he did not look uncomfortable. It was obvious he liked them as he tried to answer their questions, even when they were not listening.

As Fireman Mike sat his 6-foot 4-inch tall body in the 24-inch chair, the children sat in front of him. Each child knew his or her spot. They shuffled around his large black boots. Their eyes were glued to the firefighter who was about to read them a story. They knew the routine, even if Fireman Mike did not.

Clearly unprepared for the lesson he was to give, Fireman Mike paused to study the book he had just been given.

"Okay," he said. "This book is called *New York's Finest.*"

"Show us the pictures," shouted six-year-old Gaspare.

"Who is the author?" asked Valerie.

"Oh," said Fireman Mike, fumbling through the book to find the author.

"It's on the cover," shouted Kenny, proud to assist the behemoth man.

"Okay, okay. The author is Mary Pope Osborne. Do you know her?"

"We know her books," shouted the children. "Show us the pictures." Mike turned the book so that all the children could see the pictures. They showed him the correct way to do a read-aloud. He was getting the hang of it.

In the story, Moses Humphrey was the heroic firefighter of the 1840's. He was the toughest man in New York City and could cover an entire block with one step. He was an 8-foot tall superhero who rushed into burning buildings. He had an appetite bigger than the island of Manhattan. He saved babies and bankers alike.

"Is that you, Fireman Mike?" the children shouted.

"Nah, nah, that's not me," modest Fireman Mike said, as he turned the pages of the legend.

"It looks like you," they continued.

"Nah, nah, nah," he said.

The children listen carefully as Mike read each word aloud. They applauded at the end.

Next the children took turns trying on his fire helmet. It covered most of their heads.

"One at a time," he said. "One at a time; we have to make everyone happy."

"I want to be a firefighter," muffled the boy with red hair and freckles. The fire helmet covered his ears and nose and mouth.

Anxious to share the rest of his presentation, Mike began, "Okay, okay. Now let me give you some fire prevention tips."

"Number One," he said, lifting up one finger. "Always, always, get your parents' permission before doing anything in the kitchen."

"Number Two," he said, lifting up two fingers. "If you are ever in a fire, crawl as low as possible to the floor to escape the smoke." Then he got on the floor and crawled through the group. The children were hysterical! "This here is serious stuff," he reminded them and he went back to his tiny seat.

"Number Three," he said, "If your clothing catches fire, stop, drop and roll." He made the boy with the red hair and freckles demonstrate how to stop, drop and roll. Everyone wanted to do it but Mike said they could practice at home.

Number Four," he said with great seriousness, "Never, never, never go back into a burning building. Get out and stay out. Do you got that? Only firefighters could go into a burning building! Got it?" he asked again and again.

"Never, Never, Never!" the children repeated, shaking their heads back and forth.

"Good," he said, wiping his brow. "Okay, what number were we up to?"

"NUMBER FIVE!" the children shouted.

"Okay, okay. Let me get my train of thought. Number Five. Make sure your house has smoke alarms. They can detect fires long before you can. Go home and check!"

"Number Six," he said. "If you see fire or smell smoke, get out of your house as fast as you can."

"Number Seven," he continued. "Call the Fire Department after you are safely out of the house from a neighbor's home or cell phone. Call 911. Okay, you got that? Never go back in the house, CALL 911!" He wrote "911" very big on the board.

"Now go home and tell your parents all those tips," directed Mike. Then he reminded them of one of the most important rules of all.

"Okay now, listen up. Don't ever, ever, ever play with matches! Are you ever going to play with matches or fire?" "WE WON'T! WE WON'T! WE WON'T!" shouted the children, as they clapped for Fireman Mike.

He had done a fine job reading aloud and teaching them about fire prevention. The children adored Mike and wanted him to come back every day. When he left, he handed me a photo of himself in his firefighter uniform, standing in front of where the Twin Towers once stood. He was holding his helmet in his hands. What he was really holding was his heart. I cried.

We think you lied to us that day, Fireman Mike. You *were* the giant-sized hero in the book– the stuff legends are made of.

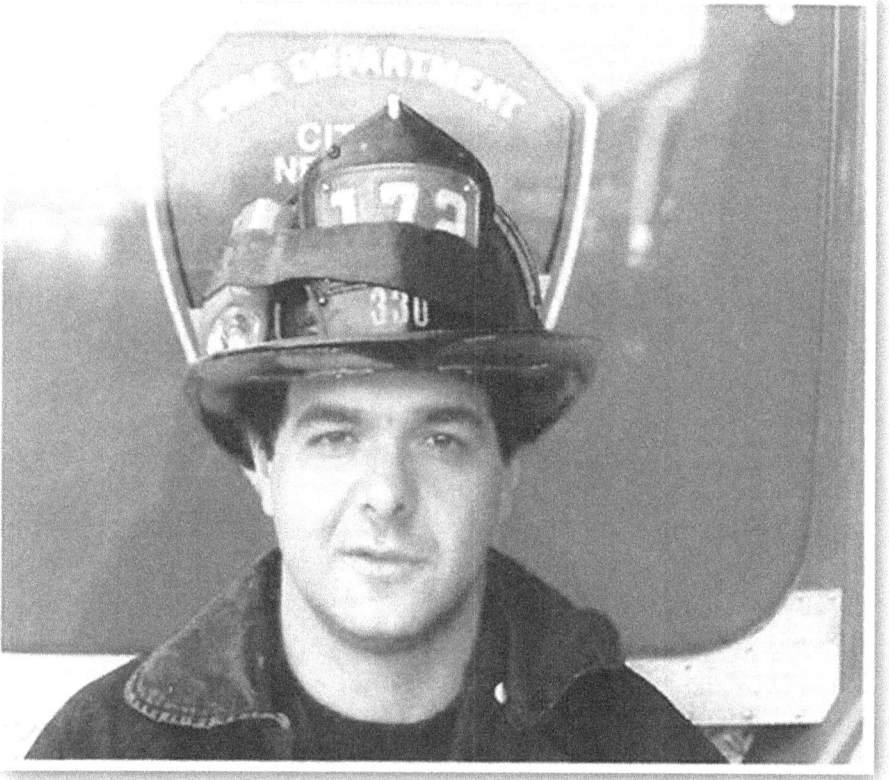

Firefighter Michael Behette, Engine 330/Ladder 172,
2312 65th Street, Brooklyn NY, 2001
A Never Forgotten Hero

The Concert for New York City
~ *Yolanda Garcia remembers*

October 20, 2001

> *"When you were young and your heart was an open book. You used to say, live and let live."*
>
> ~*Paul McCartney*

Michael was a big fan of Paul McCartney, so he was enormously pleased when it was Paul who organized *The Concert for New York City*, the benefit that took place on October 20, 2001 at Madison Square Garden to aid the victims and survivors of the 9/11 attacks. Paul brought in his contemporaries including The Who, Rolling Stones, Eric Clapton, Billy Joel, Bon Jovi, David Bowie, John Mellencamp, and others. There were also comedians and guest appearances from Mayor Giuliani, President Clinton, prominent sports figures, actors, and filmmakers. The stars signed memorabilia that was auctioned off to support foundations.

Although Michael and Yolanda had seen most of these groups before, they could not refuse the tickets, normally sold for $2,500 as a fundraiser, that were offered to them at the firehouse, gratis for a group of the guys. They went with Brian Grisanti and his wife, Cathy.

That night was not just a great collection of talents; it was an impassioned outpouring of love for New York by some of the biggest rock stars, honoring first responders, their families, those lost in the attacks, and those who had worked in the ongoing rescue and recovery efforts in the weeks since that time.

The performers played to an extremely emotional audience, crowded with victims' family members and colleagues holding up portraits of their lost loved ones.

"Michael wanted to go backstage, and of course, he found a way back there," recalls Yolanda. "With another firefighter, we were able to get through the barriers and before you know it we were there, backstage with Paul McCartney and President Clinton. Mike was prepared; he had ten photos of the icon Firefighter sitting on a stone ledge with his head lowered and his hands folded, being prayed over by an angel. He was able to ask both men, Sir Paul and President Clinton, to sign each one and they did! In exchange, he gave them FDNY t-shirts. Sir Paul really appreciated it and let everyone know that he was the son of a firefighter.

"He was amazed that these two giants' signed this one photograph ten times! Of course, Mike gave away most of the photos before the night was over, but it was still a beautiful thing," remembers Yolanda.

(Top Right) Mike with Baby James Drennen, 1997 (Top Left) T-shirt designed for fund-raising after Mike's passing
(Center) Mike with fellow firefighters and Paul McCartney at The Concert for New York City, 2001
(Bottom) Mike with brother firefighters in Florida

HE TRIED SO HARD
~ BARBARA PAGANO REMEMBERS

> *"And when the broken-hearted people living in the world*
> *agree, there will be an answer, let it be. For though they may*
> *be parted, there is still a chance that they will see....let it be"*
>
> ~PAUL McCARTNEY

"There are so many special memories that I have of Mike," remembers Barbara, "and so many that have faded over time. Some stick with us for no particular reason. It could be a smile, a laugh, a Behette-ism or some other crazy thing we did. Like the time we went camping to some Boy Scout camp with Robert, Jimmy Herro, Sam, and Clare and who knows who else came. Can't even remember the campsite anymore but do remember the details. There was quite a group of us. The girls stayed in a cabin that had opening for windows but no glass. When we woke in the morning, sitting on the windowsill was an empty beer bottle with a mouse trapped inside. I'm sure they heard my blood-curdling scream across the state!

"I yelled at Mike for putting that thing in our room. He was proud of the fact that he stuffed the mouse into the long necked bottle—stupid me, I believed him. It wasn't until one of the other guys admitted that they had found the bottle with the mouse already in it in the woods. Of course, all the guys thought it was hilarious.

"Some of my memories may seem trivial, but they are all part of my history of growing up with Mike. As we grew older, the crew started to shift, but I continued to have my traditional parties year after year.

"Super Bowl has been a tradition in my house since 1980 – an annual block party that could easily expect about 100 friends. Sometimes my family would say, 'Why can't it just be us?' But, I enjoyed having my friends over and continued to mix it up, like it or not.

"Mike always made sure that I invited him to each and every party. I wouldn't have it any other way," added Barbara.

"In 2011, I invited him to my Super Bowl party. When he said yes, I told him how excited I was, "You can't be any more excited than I am," he replied. Most of my good memories revolve around parties and the memory that touches my heart the most is the story of my son Eddie's graduation from Xaverian High School. It is a story that gives me goosebumps and makes my eyes fill with tears.

"Custom picture invitations went out to about 90 people, Mike included. The actual graduation ceremony was on June 2nd; Eddie's party was going to be at the house the following week. The night before the graduation ceremony, Xaverian has a Baccalaureate Mass for the graduates and their families at OLPH. The dean of Xaverian is an ex-cop and always arranges to have the street closed so that everyone will have a place to park. I texted Mike that day with: Come to OLPH tonight, 7PM sharp. I didn't tell him why. I just wanted him to be there and after the ceremony, I wanted him to come back to my house for coffee and cake. Mike texted back and asked where me where I was sitting. The next text asked where he could park. I texted him where we were and where he should park. I held a seat for him. The texts kept going back and forth and at 7PM the mass promptly began. I kept checking the back for his entrance and tried to discreetly text but everyone started looking at me with that look of wonder. I'm trying to whisper that I was looking for Mike. Oven a dozen texts went back and forth with the final on stating: "I CAN'T COME." I understood and knew that I would see him the next week at the party. After mass, I had to explain all my texting saying, 'Mike was coming but couldn't at the last minute.'

"After that, I didn't hear from Mike for a while, I was busy and didn't think much of it. When he didn't come to the party I knew something was wrong.

"Finally, I get a call: 'Barbara, I'm sorry I didn't come to the party but I'm at Sloan.' He said that he had started falling and at first, he was able to drag himself back up, 'You know, when I fall…I FALL.' It started happening more and more, he said, 12 to 15 times in a row. He didn't let anyone know until he fell in front of his mom. That was it. He ended up in the hospital. In Sloan, he received treatments and was expecting to get out during the week and go to rehab. 'Once I get out of rehab on Tuesday, I'll come to see you guys,' he said with such sincerity, it broke my heart.

"Tuesday came and went, and I found out he hadn't left Sloan. He kept everything to himself. Along with our friend Clare, we took a ride to Sloan to see him. At the hospital, I ribbed him about missing one of my great parties and that we missed him at OLPH.

"Outside his room, Maryann (his brother Tony's wife) approached me. 'You're the one with OLPH?' I answered yes. She explained to me that on that night, Mike was actually outside the church at 7:00. He insisted to his family that he had to go to OLPH that night. He would not tell them why. He didn't know why; I hadn't given him the details," recalls Barbara. "His family drove him there but they didn't realize they could've parked on the closed street. Instead, he insisted on being dropped off on 6th Avenue, where he attempted to walk the long avenue to the church. As he walked, they watched from the car to see him collapse to the ground, probably with his cell phone in his hand, trying to text me. They had to pick him up and put him back into the car to get him safely home. I had no idea.

"Mike was right outside the church, trying to get in to please me. He never mentioned it to me. He tried so hard. I cry to this day thinking about the drive and determination he had to do things, but mostly the love and good will he had for friends. He was unstoppable at times.

"While I was still in the hospital with him, he pulls our friend, Robert, on the side and asks him to go to the store for a graduation card to put money in it as a gift for Eddie. I was speechless. There he was lying in a hospital bed with a stent in his brain, and he was worried about a graduation gift!

"When I gave my son the gift and told him the story, he said he didn't want to spend the money; he wanted to keep it in a safe place forever. He will always treasure the card – a true testament to Mike's thoughtfulness and caring about my family.

"Mike was truly amazing and the best friend anyone could ever ask for. He was the brother I never had – without the fights. I can't remember us ever exchanging mean words. Joe and I, along with our sons, are truly blessed to have called him our friend.

"He is always in our thoughts and prayers. The suffering is over; he rests in peace with the angels."

Some Serious Business
~ *Cousin Jennifer remembers*

*"And I have one of those very loud, stupid laughs. I mean
if I ever sat behind myself in a movie or something, I'd
probably lean over and tell myself to please shut up."*

~J.D. Salinger, The Catcher in the Rye

"Oscar" and "Tony" were two very important names to Mike. He had a knack – some say a system – for predicting the winners. When the Oscar nominations were announced in January, Mike was sure to phone his cousin Jennifer and anyone else he knew would have an interest to discuss the list and who was in the running.

"Here's what you need to see," he directed Jennifer. "These are all the nominees and these are going to be the winners."

"Mike always predicted the winners, even before the nomination list came out. He let me know what movies I had to see if I hadn't already. Then I had to follow-up with him. Every week I would watch a movie and text him. We would critique the movie and make our predictions. It was very serious business. It was a way to make informed decisions about our predictions for the Oscars. Uncannily, he would call it: Best Picture, Best Actress, Best Everything! He was always right; he had a talent for it. Then during the Oscars, whenever one of his picks won, he would gloat about it! 'See, I told you. Didn't I tell you? I called it!'" Jennifer said.

Once he knew the winners, he would boast with the pride of a director, producer, and actor all rolled in one. One of his favorite picks was *Dreamgirls*. At the Academy Awards ceremony on February 25, 2007, *Dreamgirls* won the Academy Award for Best Actress in a Supporting Role and for Best Sound Mixing. It became his private mission to make sure everyone watched and enjoyed the movie about the history of Motown and The Supremes. Knowing that I was a fan of R&B music from the 1960s and 1970s, Mike insisted that I rent it and watch it. He said I would love it, and I did.

"The Oscars are hard to watch. Now I text his brother Tony and discuss what Mikey would've picked," Jennifer says. "Being with Mike was not only fun, it was an opportunity to learn lessons from Mike. He was straight-talking and practical, and he loved to share his insights and more importantly, it always came from the heart.

"Work really hard now, and make sure you have enough money put aside to travel with. When I was younger, I believed you had to get married. He told me, 'No, you don't need to get married, unless you want to.'

"What about a nice house?" Jennifer asked her cousin. "You don't need any fancy house, just a place to live. Just work hard. Don't spend all of your money and put enough away to travel and see the world. Save it all – you could then do whatever you want." It was as if he knew life was too short. He constantly reminded her, "Don't hold on to things, just go out and do stuff, even if you are by yourself."

Michael lived his philosophy. He never needed anyone to go with him anywhere. "If you want to do it, just go and do it. If you have company, great. If not, don't let that hold you back." He joked that it was easier to buy one ticket outside a concert or an event than to buy a bunch. But even if he had to buy a few, he did the best he could to get you the best seats.

Jennifer remembers how much he loved seeing Paul McCartney perform. "He followed him everywhere, was obsessed with him. He was so happy to meet him when McCartney played a concert at Madison Square Garden after the 9/11 attacks that included a line-up of superstars like Elton John, Billy Joel, Destiny's Child, and the Backstreet Boys.

It was then that New Yorkers showed their true colors because despite the line-up of superstars, one of the biggest ovations was for the 6,000 firefighters, police officers, and rescue workers honored for their heroic efforts.

It was with great pride and emotion that Billy Crystal told the crowd, "Tonight is dedicated to you." The crowd went crazy, Mike included, in his uniform blues. The audience held up pictures of those they had lost during the attacks.

The performers made the audience part of the show that night. They encouraged New Yorkers to carry on, not to live in fear, and to remember they lived in the greatest city in the world.

When the first notes of Billy Joel's *New York State of Mind* played, the crowd went wild.

Although a tragedy brought about the event, it was so uplifting and exhilarating and for Mike, a highlight in his concert career! He managed to get backstage and take a photo with Sir Paul himself!

"As a child, I wasn't as close to my Brooklyn family. I wanted to be a part of those relatives that I didn't know. When I was a teenager, I asked my Aunt Madeleine, Michael's mom, if I could come for Thanksgiving dinner. Of course she welcomed me, and that was beginning of a beautiful relationship. I bonded with all of my cousins and I learned that Michael was very protective and private about the family. He preferred never to speak about too much when it came to family matters. He was definitely overprotective. It made him uncomfortable to discuss too much."

Jennifer was happy when he finally put the seal of approval on her boyfriend, Rob. "Rob and I were together for seven years and Mike had still not met him, although he knew all about him. When they finally did meet, all I got was, 'All right, he seems okay.' That was his seal of approval," Jennifer remembers.

"The one thing that gives me consolation, despite the fact that I miss him so much, is the fact that he gets to be with his dad again in Heaven.

"'I got two suspects. You are both of them,' he would always tell me," remembers Jennifer.

A Few Words of Wisdom (or Sarcasm) from the Mind of Michael Behette

Author's Note: While interviewing Yolanda, I discovered that Michael may have had a premonition about this book. Apparently, during the last years of his life Mike was interested in having a book written about his funny stories and one-liners.

"Maybe I'll write a book. Yeah, that's a great idea," he was known to say and from that point on, all his one-liners started getting collected. "Did you get that one, Yo?" he would ask. "That was a good one right? Right? Yeah, Yeah."

He was black-and-white, simple yet extremely profound. As he said his favorite expressions, Yolanda would write them down for him. His brother, Tony, also began recording a few phrases after a lifetime of hearing them.

Here are some of those "Mike-isms," along with interpretations of their meanings by Yolanda Garcia, Marianna Randazzo and Tony Behette:

"I'll see you when I talk to you, I'll talk to you when I see you."

Typically said when he tried to get everyone together.

"You are an optimist and I am a realist, I have always been a realist. I wish I could be more like you!"

When faced with reality.

"You're an idiot." Never an insult, usually said after pranks were played on him.

"What does it all matter? It doesn't matter! Nobody cares."

He believed 30 years from now, no one would care about him. He was wrong!

"*Never mind.*"

Said when someone took too long to answer him.

"*Always look out for you. You are number one.*"

Protect your health; avoid danger zones.

"*Oh! Look at the beautiful tree!*" (*Said when someone was going to the country*)

"*Oh! Look at the beautiful rock!*" (*Said when someone was going to the Grand Canyon*)

Definite sarcasm about going to see nature. Michael preferred sightseeing, history, art, and religious journeys, such as Fatima and the Vatican.

"*Why is everyone being so nice to me?*"

He was always surprised at finding out how many people really loved him.

"*To be young and dumb again.*"

Back to youth when people didn't think or care about consequences.

"*You're too old to learn from your mistakes, so stop making them.*"

Stop acting immature.

"*Future ex-wife*"

Said to Fire Department guys who fell in love over and over again.

"*You're my super-duper last resort. Do you want to go?*"

An approach to someone who normally would decline invitations.

"*I'm in.*"

Always his response, even before a sentence was completed.

"*Write it down before you forget.*"

I'm not accepting "I forgot" as an excuse.

"*Now what?*"

What's next on the list?

"*Better to ask for forgiveness than ask for permission.*"

If you really want to do something and know they will probably say no if you ask first, you shouldn't ask. If you just go ahead and do it and they get upset, simply say it won't happen again.

"You ringa the bell; I answer the bell."
If you call me, I will come to help you.
"Everybody comes to break balls."
Self-explanatory.
"Talking to these guys is like talking to Abbott and Costello."
Can't get a clear statement from them.
"It's not about the hot tub."
When someone is upset with you over something really stupid, it's usually not about THAT at all.
"If you're interested…."
Mike would say this to someone before telling a story that may or may not be of interest to them.
"I wish I could drink like you guys."
Mike was the Best Designated Driver in the World. He would do shots, but he couldn't drink beer because it really filled him up.
"You happy now?"
Said at an awkward moment when things didn't turn out as planned.
"Don't look at me in that tone of voice."
Trying to make light of a moment when someone is upset.
"But how do they find each other?"
When Mike met people for the first time and couldn't believe how they got together.
"You worry about things that don't even exist."
Said to people who worried about or complained about things they shouldn't.

"Come on, let's go. It's not happening."
Said when Mike grew impatient and realized that it isn't going to happen, or he gave up on waiting any longer.
"I've got it down to a science."
Mike's way of saying he had it under control and to just follow his lead.
"I NEVER bothered anybody in my whole life."

Mike realizing that he may have REALLY bothered someone.

"*Mom, You are up there with Oprah and Hillary.*"

Mike always praised his mother and realized her many accomplishments.

"*Truth is stranger than fiction.*"

When Mike read a newspaper or was told a story that seemed unbelievable.

"*I am NEVER, EVER eating again.*"

Mike would always say this after he completed eating a full meal and was stuffed.

"*Our lives have been predestined by astrology, not religion.*"

Self-explanatory.

"*If he were (3 to 8 inches) taller, he would be the perfect weight.*"

Mike never called anyone fat.

"*And on the eighth day, God created Brooklyn!*"

I've had enough of you! Then he would leave!

(Top) Jimmy Herro, Gaspare Randazzo, John Olsson, Gregory Kamouh, Mike and Jimmy Olsson, in New Orleans, 2001(Bottom) Old friends at the wedding of Louie and Maria Riccardi, January 2, 2003

*(Top) Old friends since school days: Robert
Agoglia, Mike, Jimmy Herro, Gregory Kamouh (Bottom) Gaspare
Randazzo, Kevin Boyce, Sam Grillo, Gregory Kamouh and Mike*

(Top) Pat Corbett, Joi and Robert Agoglia with Mike in Seabright, New Jersey (Bottom) Hanging out with friends in Warwick, New York

WATERSKIING
~ EDDIE DESEIDERIO REMEMBERS

"We can't wait for June. We'll be gone for the
summer. We're on a surfari to stay. Tell the
teacher we're Surfin', Surfin' U.S.A...
~BRIAN WILSON, BEACH BOYS. 1963

One day and old friend, Arty Darby got a bunch of guys to go waterskiing and have lunch out on a restaurant on the water. Mike was so anxious to waterski, he began too hastily and somehow got the rope wrapped around his finger, pulling it out of joint. He was in pain, but there was no way Darby was turning back.

"The only supplies around were a pencil and some electrical tape, so I made a splint for his finger, and he had to just deal with the pain," said Eddie Deseiderio from Engine 330/Ladder 172. "Eventually we got to the restaurant for lunch. When the bill came, we told Mike he could sign for the check since he had the pencil on hand."

I'm sure he thought it was messed up and had a few choice words, but in the end it didn't matter. Mike was a good sport.

FDNY Annual Ski Race
~ Mike Besignano remembers

"Skiing combines outdoor fun with knocking
down trees with your face."

~ Dave Barry

Since 1973, Hunter Mountain has hosted the most unusual ski rac-es – the FDNY Annual Ski Race for members of the NYC Fire Department. Teams of firefighters dressed in full turn-out gear attempt to navigate through a course while carrying a 50-foot hose.

"Mike never missed the ski races. He was a great skier. Even though he grew up in Brooklyn, he always got up to the mountains for snow. His goal was to cover you in snow. I wasn't a good skier, and I'd be down in no time," remembers Mike Besignano.

Snow is slippery, and trying to balance whilst sliding down a moun-tain isn't easy, especially after strapping planks to your feet. It took a lot of confidence and that was something Mike had no shortage of. He had great control over his speed, and when he stopped, anything nearby got showered in snow. He'd slide next to you and curve the perfect turn. That massive giant of a man stopping short next you would cause an av-alanche of powdered snow to cover anything below it, especially a body lying helplessly on the ground. Mike would get such a kick out of that!

"During the races, they got a 50-foot long hose and put one guy in front and other guys every ten feet. You had to race and it was timed.

They gave prizes. My first year, I got dragged down. My foot got wrapped around a hose. Everyone was laughing at me. You hold on for dear life. Ladder 172 had Mike in the front holding the nozzle, then 10 feet later would be Dave. I was the last guy on the line. You would think it would be easy to hold on, but the truth was that the last guy got whipped around and I couldn't ski! My boots got caught. I got dragged around the mountain. It was pretty funny. At the time it was embarrassing, but now that I think about it, it was funny. There were like 100 teams – it was crazy! At night, they showed the races on a 100-inch screen while we were having beers. We'd be watching the debauchery; it was cool!" says Mike Besignano.

Eventually, Besignano learned to ski.

ALWAYS THERE ~ *JOHN SERAFINO REMEMBERS*

"It's the friends you can call up at 4 a.m. that matter."
~MARLENE DIETRICH

John Serafino will always be grateful to Mike for opening his home to him after a late night of disc-jockeying in the Brooklyn nightclubs. While moonlighting as a disc jockey, it was difficult to make his way back to his home in Long Island in the wee hours of the morning.

"Mike would frequently come out to hear me play and always offered me a place to spend the night when I got out of the clubs. Many nights, his vacant couch became my crib and those few hours were all I needed to make it home safely the next day," John Serafino recalls.

But what John will always hear in his head were all the things Mike said at the firehouse as only he could say. It was as if once he said them, they became quotes, axioms of truth, and words of wisdom. Some of his best lines were: "I like you, I'll kill you last." Or his endless question, "What do you mean by that?" Mike wanted explanations. He also let you know that he had two suspects, and they were both you. Although he denied it, one particular thing he was said to have done was to call his mother on the telephone and begin his conversation, "Hello Ma, this is Behette!" He would always argue, "I never said that!"

"Words can't express my gratitude to him and how truly blessed I feel to have known him. I will always miss my good friend, the gentle giant, Mike Behette," said John Serafino, E-330.

Paging Yolanda Garcia!
~ *Yolanda Garcia remembers*

"Picture yourself in a boat on a river, with tangerine trees and marmalade skies. Somebody calls you, you answer quite slowly, a girl with kaleidoscope eyes."

~*Lucy in the Skies With Diamonds*

"Some people may know that I have a history of missing the boat. I'm sure I'm not the only one. Every day the cruise ship's staff gets on the public announcement system to inform passengers that the ship has arrived in port and that they can go ashore. Typically, these announcements also include what time you have to be back onboard. Sometimes I have a problem with that," confesses Yolanda.

"Things happen. Cabs hit traffic; lines form in shops and check out may take longer than expected. Such was the case on our Mediterranean cruise at a port in Spain. Michael couldn't believe how late I had arrived, but I did make it back onto the ship.

"After a short while, I hear my name over the public announcement system. Not thinking I am hearing correctly, I tune in more carefully: 'Paging Yolanda Garcia. Paging Yolanda Garcia. Please come to the Captain's office. Please come to the Captain's office. There is a problem.'

"Panic stricken, I couldn't imagine why I would be called. I searched my pockets and my brain to see if I had lost anything or violated any rules. I couldn't imagine what was wrong. Michael gave me a dumbfounded look. We made our way to the Captain's office.

"The Staff Captain introduced himself and explained his role of maintaining everyone's well-being on board. He went into great detail about the complications and seriousness of missing the ship's departure. He explained how being stranded in a foreign country could be brutal and that the cruise line was not financially responsible for getting passengers to the next port if they miss the ship. I couldn't believe I was being disciplined. I was speechless.

"Suddenly, he cracked a smile and it was all over; Michael starting cracking up. I couldn't believe it! I had been duped! I don't know how he got the Captain to do this to me, but he did!

Words From the Land Down Under
~ Julian Ballard remembers

> *"What draws people to be friends is that they*
> *see the same truth. They share it."*
>
> ~C.S. Lewis

Julian Ballard, an Australian firefighter, had the pleasure of meeting Michael during the last year of Michael's life. They, along with some other good friends, Jim Olsson and John Bennett, spent some time at the Irish Pub, *The Harp*, right in the heart of Bay Ridge.

In the mixed crowd of laid-back folks looking to relax among a few friends and beers, Mike's advice to Julian was that he should be diligent about his safety and not to count on the city backing him up when things become dire. "Get regular check-ups, and try to prevent things that put you in danger," he advised.

As a fellow firefighter, Julian knew full well the dangers associated with the job, both the day-to-day risks and as was Michael's case, long-term health consequences. Julian was touched by Michael's concern and heeded his advice. But like Mike, being a firefighter is in the blood, and rescue workers sometimes follow their hearts despite their brains' warnings when it comes to what is safe or unsafe in their job and off-duty as well.

"We were hanging out in the pub and then Mike left for a while that afternoon, I wasn't sure when I would see him again," Julian remembers. "But before long, he had returned. He handed me a patch from his own uniform, and shirts and caps for my two sons. He wanted neither thanks nor gratitude. Instead he wanted me to let him know that I understood the message he was trying to give me. The message was clear. I understood. From a man who knew he was not going to get better, his compassion for others came through. I was so taken by his concern for my own health.

He truly exemplified the bond between firefighters around the world and more importantly for all mankind. It was fantastic – as was Mike."

From Belgium, With Love
~ *Tino Saitta remembers*

> *"The antidote for fifty enemies is one friend."*
>
> *~Aristotle*

Julian from Australia wasn't the only foreign firefighter with whom Michael had connected.

For eleven years, Tino Saitta, a Belgium firefighter, directed an annual crusade to New York City to honor and memorialize the heroes of 9/11, both dead and alive. Sometimes it was the mayor of Charleroi who accompanied him; other times it was doctor friends or pilots, but the delegation always included various firefighters and police officers who cherished the opportunity to pay homage to New York rescue workers, politicians, and citizens. Mike was instrumental in leading them around New York City to observe the city year after year.

Firefighter Tino Saitta remembers his first visit to Ground Zero. It was Christmastime, yet the mood in New York was one of grief and great sorrow when Tino arrived with about thirty Belgian firemen. He already knew Mike through his cousin, Gaspare Randazzo, a former New York City police officer. Mike and his fellow rescue workers appreciated the support their colleagues from across the Atlantic provided.

"Three months after the attacks, I decided to travel to the Big Apple with a colleague – to see with my own eyes. With officials' permission,

Mike allowed them access to Ground Zero. We were the first foreign firefighters to truly realize what happened there. Three months later, they were still watering the rubble. I was introduced to the Fire Chief of New York. He thanked us because we were the first foreigners to come support them. Since then, there are firefighters from around the world who come each year. I had also traveled to the place where were gathered all unidentified bodies. When I arrived on site at Ground Zero, some were still in the annex buildings at the WTC, unable to be removed as it was still chaos. With the assistance of Mike, during my visit I also met with Condoleezza Rice. The Secretary of State also came to us to thank us for the support we provide," said Tino in interviews with foreign press.

Tino kept a strong bond with Mike and for the next 10 years, neither he nor Mike missed the union between the comrades. He also remained connected with other firefighters and New York authorities. With a NYFD 9/11 bracelet permanently bolted to his wrist, Tino is the epitome of the incredible solidarity that exists among firefighters around the world.

He will forever be grateful to his cousin, Gaspare, and to Mike Behette, who arranged the meetings with Fire Commissioner Salvatore Cassano. Mike also arranged for the foreign guests to participate in some private and public displays to honor the fallen, including visits to firehouses, partaking in memorial services, entering Ground Zero, and truly being a part of the healing that helped New Yorkers. Back in Belgium, through television and media reports, Saitta shared the stories of the FDNY with the citizens of his country with admiration and respect. He was grateful to Michael for allowing him to witness and be a first-hand part of the healing process

About Cousin Michael
~ *A Poem by Gabrielle Behette*

I see him standing there outside my window in school as we sing
The Star Spangled Banner and recite the Pledge of Allegiance.
He is standing there tall among other firemen and cops.
Yet, it is only me who can see him.
What he gave me was his heart, mind and soul.
He was a great man.
I only wish he were still around
To meet all my friends and new pets.
But, now he can't.
It is still so hard for me to get over this.
He will be in my heart forever,
Watching us from the heavens and stars.
I watch him from my school window,
**We Pledge Allegiance to the Flag of the United States of America
- a country Michael loved.**

Cousin Michael was a friend, my cousin, and a hero. Everybody loved him.

He died strong with bravery. He helped after 9/11. He was such a good man. He cared about everything and everyone. But most of all, he had such a big heart, a heart that loved everyone. He had such a strong heart. I know now he loves us even more than he did on Earth.

You were a Firefighter. You fought with bravery, courage, and strength. It was amazing. You were also a cop. You had to do this with courage. This was an important job. Thank you Cousin Michael. Rest in Peace. Light the world. I love you, Michael, and everyone else loves you too.

> *"And you can tell everybody this is your song. It may be quite simple but now that it's done. I hope you don't mind, I hope you don't mind that I put down in words, how wonderful life is while you're in the world."*
>
> *~ELTON JOHN, YOUR SONG*

AM I FAT?
~ DOM GENOVESE REMEMBERS

"While riding in my Cadillac, what to my surprise. A little
Nash Rambler was following me about one-third my size....
beep, beep, beep, beep. His horn went beep, beep, beep..."

~THE PLAYMATES, BEEP BEEP. *1958*

"When I entered the firehouse for a tour, Mike asked me if I was driving. I was in E330 for a few years already. I said to him, 'As a matter of fact, I'm working in the truck today, and you are driving me.' I was the officer for that tour.

"Mike would often ask me, 'Am I fat?' My answer would always be the same. 'Yes, unless your name is Michele. Then it would be no. You never tell a woman that she is fat.'"

"Two weeks ago, when I visited Mike in the hospital, he asked me if I knew any leg exercises. I said to him, 'You must be sick! I'm the guy with the skinniest legs in the history of E330/L172,'" laughed Dom. "It was always fun to be with Mike. He had a great nature and could take the ribs, although he would probably hit you with some of his one-liners."

Dom remembers another incident several years ago when he was out with his girlfriend at a roof club bar on 5th Avenue. When he spotted Mike, he knew he could have a little fun. From his cell phone, he gives Mike a call and starts a conversation asking where he was, knowing fully well where he was. Before long, Dom hangs up and approaches Mike while continuing the conversation; Mike is still speaking into the phone. It took a while before Mike realized Dom was right behind him talking out loud. Mike's expression had to be priceless. I have great, funny memories with Mike. He was great, unselfish, warm, and a pure friend," said Dom.

Michael was known for his one-liners, Mike-isms some would call them. When he learned his cancer was terminal, his sense of humor and irony didn't stop. He often announced, "To all my friends and family, there is no hope! No cure! But I'm going to miss you!"

Imagine that, he was going to miss us.

TWICE BLESSED
~YOLANDA GARCIA REMEMBERS

"Maybe if you lived in Italy you might have the opportunity to get blessed by two different popes in one lifetime. But, how many Americans could boast such an accomplishment? Michael and I were blessed by both Saint Pope John Paul II (1978-2005) and Pope Benedict XVI (2005-2013)," states Yolanda.

"It all started when Mike and I were walking around near St. Peter's Basilica. Everyone knows that Mike could get you into any event with a pair of scalped tickets, so is it any surprise we got tickets to see the Pope?

"Michael loved hanging out in the Piazza San Pietro, directly in front of St. Peter's Basilica in the Vatican City. Michael was speaking to a street sweeper who spoke a little English when we noticed that a lot of activity was going on in the area. Michael found out from the sweeper that they were preparing for a special Papal Mass. We were very interested in attending, but you had to have a ticket to participate in a Papal Mass. Michael kept talking to his new friend, the sweeper, and before you knew it, the sweeper offered Michael two tickets. He was thrilled and wanted to pay for them, but the sweeper refused. He said the tickets were free and he couldn't use them, so he was happy to give them away. Since it is recommended to arrive one to three hours before the mass begins, we were already on time!

It was a Solemn High Mass, with the Pope's entrance into St. Peter's Square accompanied by a fanfare of silver trumpets. Processions were led by the cardinals, bishops, and priests according to ranks.

Years later, we went back to Rome and were among the audience in St. Peter's Basilica. The Pope appeared, said prayers, and gave blessings and a homily. Perched high above the thousands of people are signs with the words ENGLISH, SPANISH, FRENCH, POLISH, and various other languages, written boldly for the Pope to see. One by one, the Pope recited a blessing in each of the languages represented. We had been blessed by two popes in one lifetime!

One of Mike's favorite places in the world was the Trevi Fountain in Rome. For him, it was a fantastic work of art – so much more than a mere sculpture. The sounds of the gushing waters could be heard from nearby streets. At the fountain, I made the same one wish every time we were together; I wished that Michael and I would be together forever. Through the years, we had been apart, but when we were together, it was only us.

FROM ONE HERO TO ANOTHER
~ JOHN GRAZIANO REMEMBERS

"We can be heroes, for ever and ever. What d'you say?"

~DAVID BOWIE, HEROES

FDNY Captain John Graziano*

"There are many sides to this incredible person we've all come to know and love as Mike Behette. He was a dedicated and great firefighter, as well as a loving and caring man who can always be counted on when the chips are down and you are in need of a friend. He was also a very private person who wanted his personal life kept just that way.

"I remember when he was first diagnosed; he didn't want anyone to know because he didn't want to be treated differently than at any other time. When I first offered to take him to his doctor appointments, he refused and said not to worry, he was just fine. But, I looked him dead in the eye and said to him, if the situation were reversed and I was sick who would be the first person at my door looking to help me out? He looked me in the eye and smiled letting me know he'd be there for me if it were me instead of him. No surprise to me, because if you knew Mike, you knew he was there for everybody in his life who was in need of help. He was undoubtedly one of the most caring and loving individuals I've ever met. If you needed him, he was there, unquestionably and unflinching, truly an amazing guy.

"Seventeen years ago when my mother was terminally ill, he came to the firehouse one day and gave me holy water that he brought back from Lourdes in a statue of the Blessed Mother. He told me he didn't know if it would cure her disease, but he believed it would help her spiritually. I'll never forget the kindness he showed my family in our time of need.

"It has been a privilege and an honor to serve in the FDNY with Mike, but is an even greater privilege and honor to have been a part of his life and to have had him as a friend for nearly 30 years! To know him was to love him!"

Retired FDNY Captain John Graziano, formerly of Ladder 78, died on Friday, March 13, 2015 of World Trade Center—related pancreatic cancer.

In 2001, Graziano was a lieutenant at Brooklyn's Ladder 132 Engine 280. The Prospect Heights Company lost seven members in the attacks. The days immediately following September 11th were spent working at the site, searching for friends and co-workers, and then burying them.

"The firehouse actually got stronger. I mean, everybody was really aggrieved and sorrowful over the loss of our loved ones, but it actually brought everybody closer. Everybody pulls together," said Graziano.

(Top) Mike with fellow firefighters. (Bottom) Mike with Mayor R. Giuliani, 2001, Mayor of New York City, 1994-2001

(Top) Mike speaking with President Clinton at Concert for New York, 2001 (Bottom) Mike with his cousin Joey Behette

(Top) Ladder 172, Bensonhurst
(Bottom) Hanging out with Robert DeNiro

One More Night of Fun
~ *Arlene VanDyk Coyle remembers*

"So I was the one with all the glory, while you were the one with all the strain. A beautiful smile to hide the pain."

~ *Bette Midler, Wind Beneath My Wings*

" **M**ichael was the only guy that I kept in touch with after high school. We did a lot of things together – concerts, Yankee games, etc. We would watch movies, meet and walk along the bicycle path, and just meet up for lunch or dinner," recalls Arlene.

"Our last conversation had been at Christmastime and I decided to give him a call to go out for St. Patty's Day. It was that time of the year. We had a wonderful night and laughed a lot.

"The next morning he called me. Living in Bay Ridge, there's not much that stays quiet. He wanted to tell me that he had cancer, but wanted to have fun the night before. He thought we should have one more good night out! We cried for about an hour afterwards. That was so typical of Michael, and I will never lose that memory. To allow me to enjoy another night with him before we had to deal with his illness was the most selfless act, and I loved him so much for it. There are so many funny memories of him but that is a true testament of who Michael was. I miss him every day, and his picture is on my wall to remind me that he will always be in my heart," said Arlene.

Arlene believes that Michael still intercedes in her life; he is a true guardian angel.

Fatima
~ *Yolanda Garcia remembers*

"Give me an army saying the Rosary
and I will Conquer the world."

~*Pope Blessed Pius IX*

"On our second trip to Europe, we flew into Rome for a few days before continuing on a cruise to Lisbon, Portugal. Once there, we tried to find an excursion to Fatima, an important Catholic shrine dedicated to the Virgin Mary that is visited each year by millions of people from all over the world. We were surprised that we couldn't find one, but undeterred, we arranged our own. Michael employed a cab driver for 200 euros to take us on the two-and-a-half hour trek to Fatima. We invited others to join us, but no one wanted to embark on the journey with us. When we returned, they regretted not going and asked us to share some of the religious articles with them. We each bought about 30 pairs of rosary beads for our family and friends, and gave away about half of what we bought to the people we dined with on the cruise.

"In Fatima, we gathered in Cova da Iria, an enormous plaza where a little chapel was built and where the Virgin Mary is believed to have appeared to three young children six times in 1917. In the Basilica were the tombs of two of the three children who had visions of the Virgin Mary. They were the brother and sister, Francisco and Jacinta, who died

187

in 1919 and 1920 respectively, as the Blessed Mother had foretold. We learned that they were beatified in 1970. One grave remained for the third child, their cousin Lucia, who was still alive at the time. We had our cab driver take us to Lucia's house in the hopes that she would make a slight appearance, but she did not. It was said that she led a life of seclusion and prayer and only spoke to the Pope. Sr. Lucia dos Santos died in 2005; she was 97 years old.

"We bought candles to burn in the sanctuary, to participate in the ceremony of candles. We saw the bush that is now a tree, where the Blessed Mother appeared. It is now beautifully landscaped with pavers, and the sacred tree is surrounded by a wall about two-feet tall," remembers Yolanda.

A Boy and a Man
~ *Blake Appleton remembered*

Far from Brooklyn in Lake Wales, Florida, a little boy very much like Michael lived his life to the absolute fullest and did not let anything get in the way of that. He had set goals for himself and went about attaining them. One of his many dreams was to reach out to NFL quarterback Tim Tebow, which he did. Another was to visit New York City with his mom and his sister. He also had aspirations of becoming a firefighter, so who better than to be his tour guide and eventual hero than an actual NYC firefighter in the city of the majestic Empire State Building?

Blake Appleton was five years old when he declared he wanted to be a fireman. "So I can save people's houses when they were burning down," declared Blake. His dream was halted in 2008, when doctors discovered a large tumor embedded in his brain. He underwent multiple surgeries, along with numerous rounds of chemotherapy and radiation treatment.

In a feature story published in Lakeland, Florida's *The Ledger*, Blake said he eventually chose to cease further treatments "because I wanted to be a fun kid." He had dreams that needed to be fulfilled. The beautiful boy with the contagious smile had the opportunity to meet Tim Tebow, then the quarterback of the Denver Broncos before an actual Broncos game. "He said I'm his hero," Blake told *The Ledger*, after his adventure.

Blake was in the second grade at Polk Avenue Elementary School in Lake Wales until he decided to stop attending in March. The school honored him with a "Leader of Courage" award. His next dream was to go to NYC. There were people he needed to see and places that he needed to visit.

A friend of Blake's mom, Miranda was a first responder in New York City. A friend of her friend was a woman named Linda who set up activities for the NYC Fire Department. It was Linda who arranged for Blake to meet Michael at a breakfast for World War II veterans. Somehow, Linda who was also friends with Michael and knew that brave Blake and Michael would hit it off during his visit to the Big Apple and *The New York Transit Museum*. Where else could a boy who loved trains get to see the historical artifacts of the New York City subway, bus, commuter rail, and bridge and tunnel systems? Michael was anxious to meet Blake as well, so the two women touched base.

"It couldn't hurt for these two courageous guys to meet. Michael, a real NYC firefighter and a victim of cancer and little Blake who had been battling brain cancer for four and half years," said Miranda, "If his story could inspire an adult, why not?"

On the day they met, Blake wasn't feeling well; his runny nose was acting up with his sinus problems. The two met at the WWII veteran's breakfast somewhere in Brooklyn. In a playful way to help him forget about his sniffles, Michael started playing with his cherub cheeks and soon Michael had him laughing. "Before long, the two of them were cutting it up, playing with each other. When they discovered their mutual love - baseball. - Michael knew he had found a new best friend! It was the beginning of a beautiful friendship. Next stop was a day at the *New York Transit Museum* with Blake, his mom, and sister. They went in and out of the subway cars, Mike pushing Blake in his stroller when he was too tired to walk. Then in true Uncle Mikey fashion, the gentle giant treated the kids to souvenirs, t-shirts, snacks, and goodies all day long. They both shared a love of the trains that were displayed in the museum for all of New York to admire and reminisce about. Blake admired the antique New York trolleys and buses in awe, while Michael remembered the trains of his youth.

It was a beautiful day for Michael and Blake! For one day they got to forget they were sick and they both lived for the moment. To add to the thrill of the day, they visited the control room in Brooklyn at Metro Tech. It was there Michael showed nine year-old Blake how it all got done. He watched with his own eyes as first responders dashed to fires and medical emergencies. He witnesses firsthand how the FDNY protected the lives and property of New York City residents and visitors. For Michael, it must've have been like reliving his days of glory with the FDNY. A man and a boy living in the moment.

Blake's mom, Miranda shared, "When we returned, it was all Blake could talk about. On top of that, Linda was making arrangement for us to go back to New York to attend a New York Yankees game with Michael. It was never to happen. Blake became more ill and seizures prevented him from traveling. Blake passed away in May of 2012. Not long after that, Michael passed away. Now they are both watching the Yankees from heaven, front row seats," said Miranda.

To honor his legacy, *The Blake Appleton Foundation* has been established. It a nonprofit organization whose main purpose is providing toys and other gifts to terminally ill children.

(Top) Mike with his two nieces, Daniella and
Allison, at a party celebrating his life
(Bottom) Mike with Blake Appleton, a brave little boy from Florida

Calvary
– *John Albano remembers*

At the end, when Michael was in the hospital, John Albano's only regret was that he hadn't kept more in touch with his old pal. "He never had problems with anyone. I should've made an effort to see him more. But what really impressed me the most was the care Mike had in the hospital. I don't think I would ever get such care.

While he was cared for at *Calvary Hospital Hospice* in Brooklyn, his mother, brother, sisters, relatives, and friends were always at his side. If one person walked away, another member took his place. I sat in rooms with relatives I never met and shared hugs and treats. Seeing Mike, a mythical-sized strong guy, so fragile and vulnerable was heartbreaking. He had the way of making strangers hug in solidarity for him. They all accepted me and made me feel welcome, even though all those years had passed. His mother, of course, remembered me from all those years ago. Because of our loss, so many friends reconnected – even kids I played football with when we were 13 years old!"

This is My Sister, Marguerite

*"And it seems to me you lived your life like a
candle in the wind…and I would've like to have
known you but I was just a kid. Your candle
burned out long before your legend ever did."*

~ELTON JOHN, CANDLE IN THE WIND

In the days in the end when countless family members and friends
stood vigilantly by Michael's bedside at Lutheran's Calvary Hospital,
so many friends had discovered Marguerite Behette for the first time.

It surprised her that so many friends didn't know Mike had a sister,
as most were acquainted with his brother, Tony. But those who knew
Mikey well knew that he often kept the things and people most precious to him private. Such was the case with his sister Dr. Marguerite
Behette and her daughter and two sons, whom Mike adored. Mikey was
also uncle to Tony's girls, and as one neighbor, Dennis Pappas, recalls,
"Mike was a great uncle to Daniella and Allison. I often told him, 'I wish
you were my uncle!'"

Marguerite's kids were the next generation in the Behette clan – full
of life, joy, and spunk. They kept Uncle Mikey on his toes, and he kept
them on a pedestal while he showered them with love, affection, and
lots of the toys they still cherish.

Today, her children will tell you that on September 11, 2001, their Uncle Mikey was on a cruise ship in Florida, rented a car and defied the law to race home to help people. They will tell you that he was one of the many heroes of that day. But most importantly, they will tell you that in their eyes, Uncle Mikey was a hero every day of their lives.

Each one of these three beautiful children possess a part of Michael that has been indelibly placed in their souls from the love and attention he showered them with during the years he was part of their lives. The oldest, William, is a bright, inquisitive young man with a zest for knowledge who is as intrigued and fascinated by life as his uncle was. Each year, he presented his uncle with a list of museums he wished to attend. Together they explored and experienced the historical, scientific, artistic, and cultural wonders of the universe.

Anne, the beautiful, graceful dancer inherited a love of theater, performances, and the arts. Her She is a free spirit, endowed with the gifts for singing, dancing, and acting – all the things her Uncle Mikey greatly appreciated. There is no doubt that he will be guiding this young lady as she blossoms into a talented performer.

Little Thomas, the rough-and-tumble little boy with a collection of trucks, cars, emergency vehicles (mostly purchased by Uncle Mikey), will tell you there is only one thing he wants to be – a Fireman. Perhaps it was all those trips to the local firehouse where Uncle Mikey took the five year-old boy to climb into the fire truck or hang out with the guys long after his own firefighter days had ended that embedded the dream in his little nephew. The dream his Uncle Mikey once had as a boy himself.

These were Mikey's surrogate children, spoiled and loved until the end and then some.

The Behette Family through the years

New Connections
~ Marianna Randazzo remembers

> *"Dear Sir or Madam, will you read my book? It took me years to write. Will you take a look?"*
>
> ~J. Lennon/P. McCartney, Paperback Writer

"While visiting Michael in the hospital, I got to see so many friends my husband and I hadn't seen in years, as well as all of Michael's family," recalls Marianna. We already knew Tony. We had hung out with him and his wife, MaryAnn, over the years and had attended concerts together. But the biggest surprise was meeting Michael's lovely sister, Marguerite – Dr. Marguerite Behette. Imagine how shocked we were to find out Mike had a great sister like that, and that she was an ophthalmologist! You'd think he would've mentioned it! Also during those visits, I had the pleasure of meeting Michael's aunts and cousins. Small world that it is, it turned out that I had worked with Giselle and Salwa over the years when I was a staff developer in District 20. Of course, the most interesting person I met during those visits was Madeleine. As she clung to her faith and prayers, we discussed God's love and her devotion to her saints and the Lord. And we prayed for miracles.

"The firefighters who flowed in and out of the hospital were phenomenal. They came between shifts from all over the city and provided a family transport vehicle for the family.

After Michael's death, the Behette family and Mike's Ladder company donated a Fire Family Transport Vehicle in his memory so that other families should be comforted and accommodated during difficult times.

As we hung out with each other in the room, Mike would always chime in proving that he had never lost his funky sense of humor. At the time, my first book, a biography, had been published and we talked about the book. He told me he was happy for me, but after a few minutes, his voice became weaker. In keeping with his true spirit, his last few words to me were 'Maybe you can write a book about me one day.' 'Why not?' I answered."

Bubbles for Bubbles
~ John Albano remembers

*"Tiny bubbles, in the wine, make me feel
happy. Ah! They make me feel fine."*

~Leon Pober, Tiny Bubbles

Underneath it all, Mike was a hopeless romantic. John Albano confirmed this when he stated that one of Mike's favorite old films was *My Favorite Brunette* with Peter Lorre, Dorothy Lamour, Lon Chaney, and Bob Hope, a romantic comedy about a baby photographer on death row in San Quentin State Prison who tells reporters his story.

It was Christmastime and John had watched the movie and thought of his old pal. He went to Greenwood Cemetery, where Mike was buried, to visit his friend for Christmas. Along the way, he stopped and bought the supersize bottle of Miracle Bubbles with the Miracle Wand inside. "I went to visit his gravesite and I left the bottle of bubbles on his grave with a note that said, 'Blow a Bubble for Bubbles!' Later on that day, I got a telephone call from Giselle, Michael's cousin, which made me very nervous. She said that Madeleine, Mike's mom, wanted to speak with me. "I got very upset because I was afraid that maybe they took it as an insult and that was the last thing that I ever wanted. I hoped that they didn't take it wrong. It was meant as a nice thought.

"Before I got to call her back, she had called my house while I was out and left a message on my machine. In her distinct Syrian accent, she left me this message: 'Hello John, this is Michael's mother, Madeleine. John, I will never forget what you did for my son, and every time that I go, I will blow a bubble for Bubbles!' Relieved and happy to hear her message, I called her back and we spoke for over 40 minutes," said John.

Thanks for the memories, Mike.
We truly miss you.

Thanks for the Memories

*"Awfully glad I met you. Cheerio. Tootle-
oo. Thank you, thank you."*

~Bob Hope & Shirley Ross, *Thanks For The Memory*.

Susan Olsson: What pops into my head is that he always made an effort to come to my children's affairs and he was extremely generous. I admired him for showing up and always making an effort. Michael also genuinely like children and was very kind to my own children. As they got older, he especially took Johnny under his wing and was truly proud of their accomplishments. We met over thirty years ago through my husband, John, and a group of us have been friends all of those years. We've been together through good times, lots of parties, sad times, sicknesses and funerals, traveling, Jets games and, of course, our famous New Orleans trip where 60 close friends got together for a Jets game!

Marianna Randazzo: On March 2, 2012 at a restaurant called *Giando's*, we had a party for Mike. It was bittersweet. That night we ate and drank and listened to our favorite music while admiring the skyline of Manhattan. A fun photo booth was available where friends couldn't stop taking pictures with Michael. Dressing him up with boas and other props, Michael laughed with the rest of us, hopefully forgetting his pain for one night. Wearing his "I have two suspects..." t-shirt, he posed all

*Marianna Randazzo and Mike at the Engagement Party
of her daughter Valerie and Kenny, October, 2011*

night with friends and family, young and old. Topped off by an enormous display of candies, cookies and treats, a good time was had by all.

Through the window wall overlooking the East River, we watched while a firefighter tugboat ceremoniously drifted by to salute Michael and display fantastic fireworks, He was touched by how many friends he truly had. We laughed and cried. He told us he would miss us; he had it the wrong way.

It was all a perfect recipe for beautiful memories.

Michael never missed an occasion. Every year he showed up at the Randazzo Christmas party, even though he probably had a half-dozen other invitations. He also probably attended them all. The year that he passed, I knew he was not feeling well and didn't expect him to attend my daughter and son-in-law's engagement party. Just as we got started, in walks Mike. That night he stayed for the whole party. We were happy to have him there.

Gerry Quinn: Mike Behette, aka "The Gentle Giant," was one of the kindest, caring and warm-hearted human beings I have ever met. It was an honor and a privilege to work with Mike. His big heart shined brightly when it came to mutual. Mike was the mutual broker of E-330 L-172.

He would take it upon himself to try and help every firefighter get the tours they needed off, even though the Officers and Battalion 42 Aides would break pencils over his efforts!

I saw Mike many times during his last assignment at the World Trade site. He never complained about being there. He was proud to help. L-172 was a better truck company with Mike Behette on the riding list. He knew when to kick it up a notch, and we all knew he could tone it down when needed.

I consider myself blessed to have had the opportunity to meet such a wonderful human being and a great firefighter.

Frankie Zulferino, E330: I worked with Mike for 11 years. Mike was a big teddy bear, and a stand-up guy. But you didn't want to get Mike mad. I would always say, 'One day someone going to piss him off and he's going to come into the Firehouse, pick up an ax and chop everyone up.' But, of course, that was firehouse talk.

Mike was a great man and a friend to all, as everyone could see, by the amount of people who showed up at the hospital to visit him on a daily basis.

I remember when Mike was diagnosed with this terrible cancer. He called me, asking me questions about the cancer. Mike knew my brother passed away from this same cancer in 2007 at the age of 47. I remember telling Mike to stay positive, new drugs are coming out all the time and everyone responds differently. Mike put up a great fight and showed tremendous courage throughout his battle.

Mike, you were the public relations man for all the retired guys. If it weren't for you, myself and others wouldn't know half the things going on. You were the glue that kept everyone together. You will be missed by all, and I will sincerely miss you, my friend.

Mike Bacigalupo: Mike, I love you, man! You have always been there for me in the past. You've always stepped up. I've been impressed by you at jobs while at 172. I have seen you make rescues, even two at one time!

You did some creative firefighting, even one classy interview with Larry King at WTC. Brother, you're the only guy I know who could line up a 14-way mutual and pull it off without a hitch! You're the man! Working with you was the best. Brother, just letting you know you're always on my mind.

Deanna Drew: Mike was a wonderful friend of mine for 19 years. I met Mike on my first date with one of Mike's best buddies. Years later, when I was living in Florida, my sister and I returned to New York and when we saw Mike, he said to me in his famous drawn out sentence, "IIII'll really miss you!" It melted my heart, and I knew those words were as genuine as the man that he was. Our last day together was spent at Yankee Stadium and it was truly priceless. Despite being very sick, he was determined to make our first visit to the new stadium memorable and it certainly was.

Jacki Wanagiewicz: What a kind and gentle soul you still are! I remember going camping to Spruce Pond in Upstate New York and the amazing times we used to have. You are a teardrop in my eye. I will always remember the fun we had – never a dull moment with you around!

You are daily missed.

XOX

Gloria Harris: About twenty years ago, a guy named Larry Lundy was hit by a car on Third Avenue and 87th Street in Brooklyn. Mike was in the bar/restaurant on that corner, and he immediately ran out when he heard the commotion. Larry was lying unconscious on the ground when Mike sprang into action. Without hesitation he performed mouth-to-mouth resuscitation and revived him. He saved his life. Eventually, an ambulance arrived and took him off to the hospital. Michael springing into action was typical of his nature.

This man Larry, that Michael saved, was a family friend. Whenever I think of Mike, I remember what a good fireman he was, springing into action, but he was also a wonderful human being with a good heart. He showed compassion for all people. With every fire truck that passes, Michael Behette comes to my mind. We need more people like him in this world.

Please shine on me always.

Jen Cannava: There's so many stories! Mike was more than a friend he was like family. He was my Uncle Arthur Darby's best friend. My Aunt Kathy and Uncle Arthur have been friends with Mike for years. I remember Mike being around my family since I was a baby. The last time Mike was in Florida we all went to see him in Miami. He was sick at this time with the tumor in his neck but it did not stop him from having fun and enjoying Miami to the fullest. We rented scooters and drove all around South Beach. Then we went to one of his favorite places, *The Clevelander* in South Beach. We had an amazing day to remember. Mike was always happy and always wanted people to have a good time! He did everything for people. I truly miss him he was a great soul. I'm so happy to have shared so many great memories with him.

Yolanda Garcia: Having been with Michael for over ten years already, I was quite familiar with his ways. I believe I really tested Michael's patience on my daughter's wedding day. I warned him that it would be a long day and that there was only one car, no way out! He assured me he would be there for us all day long, and he was. It was a special day for both of us, as he had also seen my daughter grow up. He was with us from the bridal dress-up shoots to the last dance at the reception. I'm sure he had a great time; he danced all night with friends and it was great to have him by my side.

WALL OF HONOR: COLORADO SPRINGS

The International Association of Fire Fighters (IAFF) Memorial, located in Colorado Springs, was founded to recognize and honor past and future professional fire fighters and emergency medical personnel who are killed in the line of duty and to provide assistance to the surviving spouses and children of those members.

The bronze likeness of a firefighter "Somewhere, Everyday" epitomizes the courage and bravery displayed daily by professional fire fighters across the continent. Granite Wall of Honor bears the names of fallen IAFF members. The names of brothers and sisters killed in the line of duty have been etched there each year since 1986. Although thousands have died throughout our union's history, the names on these walls date back only through 1976, when the U.S. federal government first began tracking line-of-duty deaths in the fire service.

Each September, the IAFF conducts an annual Fallen Fire Fighter Memorial Observance to honor the sacrifice made by professional fire fighters and paramedics who have given their lives in the line of duty during the previous year.

On September 21, 2013, Michael Behette's name was added to the Wall of Honor.

Internet Tribute to Michael
~ John Mitchell

During a random search on the Internet, Michael Behette's name came up on the Fire Engineering website blog penned by John Mitchell, a Chicago firefighter and paramedic since the 1970s. John is the President of Diamondplate Productions, and has served as a department training officer and college lead instructor for state firefighter and EMS courses. John also responds to national disasters across the country as a member of the FEMA's Command Staff in External Affairs.

I immediately wrote to John, thanked him for writing about Michael, and told him about this book. I requested permission to reprint his editorial. This was his response to me:

> *Hello, Marianna.*
>
> *After the Navy Yard shootings, I penned a brief article for my blog "Fire Daily" recounting your friend, Mike Behette, and the heroic way he lived his life. I applaud your efforts in continuing to spread the word on Mike's life. Firefighters worldwide are proud to count Mike as one of us forever. God bless!*

This is the content of that blog entry:

We Should Be Hearing All About Mike Behette Today, Rather Than Knowing So Much About the Navy Yard Shooter.

Posted by John Mitchell on September 17, 2013 at 11:42 a.m.
Here we go again.

By now, we know way too much about the coward with anger management issues who killed a dozen innocent people yesterday at the DC Navy Yard. I won't repeat his name.

Someone said he never got over "his demons" working at Ground Zero immediately following the 9/11 attacks. Boy, that sure sucks, eh?

In my opinion, we give these criminals way too much coverage. They don't deserve our attention. I'll keep it clean here: "Screw them."

Instead, I propose we direct our attention to someone else who worked The Pile on September 11th. A good guy. A great guy.

He is our Brother Mike Behette. An FDNY firefighter assigned to Ladder 176 in Bensonhurst until his 2002 retirement, Mike was diagnosed with lung cancer in 2011.

This cancer is a direct result of Mike's bravery, serving valiantly at Ground Zero immediately following the cowardly attack on our country. Since then, the cancer spread to his brain and spine.

Mike was vacationing in Florida when he heard that the twin towers had been hit by hijacked planes.

Unable to fly to New York, the Dyker Heights resident rented a car and, getting speeding tickets on his way, drove until he reached his destination: the wrecked scene at Ground Zero.

He worked The Pile for over a month afterwards, digging up and cleaning debris and continued working at the scene for six continuous months, searching desperately for his missing colleagues.

Mike passed away one year ago today. He was 55.
Let's give him more attention today. He deserves it.
Never forget those still dying.

Signs From Michael

*G*iselle and Dawn Get a Message. There is no doubt that Michael brought people together. Whether it was a Jet's game, a Thanksgiving Day parade or New Year's Eve, it gave him great pleasure to have friends and relatives meet and become friends. Such was the case between his godchild Giselle Awad and Dawn Bergen.

Giselle recalls, "After Michael passed, Dawn and I decided to spend a few days in the Hamptons. It was one of the first times that we hung out without Mike. We passed a Farmer's Market and a church. They dated back over a century and sort of set up the scene. Suddenly, we spot a man sitting on the grounds strumming a guitar, or maybe it was the sitar – the Indian instrument used by the Beatles. As we passed, he silently hummed the words to *"Norwegian Wood (This Bird Has Flown)."* We stopped and listened. He followed it up with *Let it Be*. With tears in our eyes, Dawn and I knew that this was Mike's way of letting us know he was happy our friendship had become what it was."

Since *Let It Be* was the last album the Beatles released, it made an appropriate statement about leaving problems behind and moving on in life. Of course, anywhere you go in the world, you will hear Beatle music, but for Giselle and Dawn, it was a sign.

Valentine's Day - Thursday, February 14, 2013. Madeleine shared this story: "Five months after my son was gone, it was Valentine's Day – a day my son never forgot me. On this day, I went into the basement, as I needed to find an address of one of my Salesian nuns that I still communicate with. In searching for the address, I pick up a plastic bag. It wasn't a bag I had remembered placing there on the table. It just seemed to appear. Do you know what I found in it? It was note from my Michael. 'Mom, I was here and you were not.' I started crying and calling for him, hoping that somehow he could appear to me. 'Michael, where are you?' I cried. The letter continues, 'Life is like a box of chocolates. You never know what you are going to get. Love, your wonderful son, Michael.'

"I was so scared; I felt like he was there with me, telling me to enjoy Valentine's Day and remember what he left behind. How could I ever forget?" his heartbroken mother remembers.

Mother's Day, Sunday, May 12, 2013. Any parent who has suffered the loss of a child knows the pain of marking holidays without them, especially the first time. For Madeleine, on the first Mother's Day after Michael's death, she was filled with grief and sorrow and a feeling of no longer being complete.

"I decided to go to my sister's house and my niece, Gisele, tells me that something amazing was posted on Facebook. It seems that Jimmy Olsson had discovered a picture of a Patrolman Behette. He wanted to know if there was a relationship to me. Of course, it was my husband, George, as a Patrolman in 1958! I remembered the incident. He and his partner had rescued two children and the photograph appeared in the newspaper. Jimmy had posted it on Facebook. I had not seen that picture in 55 years. Here it is, Mother's Day, and a photo of my husband surfaces! Was it Michael telling me he was with his dad and was okay? It was an unbelievable coincidence that I would receive this picture on Mother's Day. I believe it was a gift from my son," recalls Madeleine.

N.Y.C. Newspaper article, May 16, 1958.
Brooklyn, New York: Cops console Abandoned Tots. Ptl. George Behette, left
holds Anna Marie Gionala, 3, as Ptl. Frank Compitello holds her brother,
Mike, 2, in the Bergen Street station today. The patrolmen found the two
children on the first floor of a rooming house at 75 Eight Avenue this after-
noon. Police are searching for the mother, Mary who left the tots in a fur-
nished room at 1:00P.M. today. (Reprinted with permission from Corbis)

Michael's Birthday - June 24, 2013. Marking special occasions is especially painful for a grieving heart. Madeleine tried to honor Michael and keep his memory alive by visiting his grave. "My grandchildren had not been to the cemetery to see Michael since his passing. My granddaughter Ann insisted that we go on the exact day of his birthday. Thomas, the youngest, only five at the time, started asking many questions. 'Is Uncle Mikey here?' he wanted to know, as he solemnly stood in front of the gravesite and made the Sign of the Cross.

"The weather started changing, looking like rain. Marguerite started back to the car with the three children. I had asked for two more minutes to be alone in prayer with my son.

"Suddenly, a bird started towards us, 'Look, look!' she pointed it out to me, but then she shooed it away. The bird took off and went into a big tree, hiding itself among the branches so it was no longer visible. She tried again to go back to her car, and I again tried to spend two more minutes with my son. "As I prayed, the little bird appeared again in front of me on the grave. The children ran out again to look at the creature. Just as the oldest, William, approached, it flew directly into his hand. I had never seen such a friendly bird – one that came towards people, one that did not fly away! We sat on the floor and played with the bird. He was not injured, and we had seen it fly away the first time. Despite its free will, it did not leave us! It brought us all such joy. 'Well, Marguerite,' I said. 'I guess we are taking him home.' We took it into the car. Oddly enough, it sat among us without attempting to leave. It did not fly, did not flutter. On the way home, we stopped at the pet shop to buy supplies. The man told us our yellow bird was a parakeet.

"I believe I heard Michael in my heart that day. He saw how happy he had made us. I believe he just wanted us to be joyful, and we were.

"The bird came home with me. We name him Michael. When the children come over, the first thing they ask is, 'How's Mike?' Chirp, chirp, Mikey is fine," said Madeleine, with a smile.

Michael's Birthday - June 24, 2014. "The temperature was in the 80s and Marguerite's children had not been feeling well. I was concerned," stated

Madeleine. "I preferred that they stayed home. Yet, she and they wanted to visit Michael at the cemetery to honor him on his birthday. We had decided to take two cars in case there was a need to change plans.

"Earlier that day, I had spoken to Dawn Berger. Dawn always honors Michael with masses at church, and she had called me as she often does. 'Wouldn't it be something if Michael sends you another gift of nature on his birthday?' Dawn tells me, referring to my bird that I have at home. 'Yes, that would be something,' I agreed.

"Marguerite and the children were following me to the cemetery. She had decided to leave them in the car with the air conditioner on that hot day. I spent some time praying at the grave, but of course, I was more preoccupied with my grandchildren's health.

"On the way back, near 4th Avenue and 78th Street. (The cemetery is Greenwood, located at near 5th Avenue and 25th Street.) Marguerite stopped her car, and I did also. She stopped to check the children and was now out of her car. Standing on the sidewalk near a row of stores, she spotted a bird that walks directly to her. She is quite astonished, and knew it was a bird that was meant to come home with us. She quickly enters a nearby laundromat and exits with a clothes hanger. The little bird walked itself onto the hanger and into our hearts. Again, like the first one, it was a gift from Michael to us! On his birthday, he continues to give us gifts.

"I brought the little parakeet into my car where he sat in the passenger seat, and I opened the window enough for him not to get overheated. I did not want the air-conditioned to blow directly on him.

"Back in the neighborhood, I visited the same pet store on 4th Avenue and 93rd Street, where I explained my bird stories to the man in *Fins, Furs and Feathers* pet shop. The gentleman examined him and pointed out that his beak was a bit injured, but he wasn't concerned about it. After he heard my story, he widened his eyes and lifted his arms up to the heavens.

"Bird Number Two came home with me, and both remain in my home. They are signs that Michael is always with me!" remarks Madeleine.

*(Top) Remembering Michael Fundraiser for Firefighter's
Family Transport Vehicle at Indigo Murphy's Bar, Bay Ridge, Brooklyn
(Bottom): Family visiting the cemetery and receiving a surprise visit*

Yolanda Garcia believes that Michael has also been with her spiritually especially when she needed a guiding hand. She shared this story: "After a few months in the Bahamas with my children and grandson running the family diving business, it was time to return home to New Jersey. We drove the boat to West Palm Beach, Florida where our car was parked while we were away. Although it was 3 a.m., it was decided that I would drive the first leg of the journey back, while everyone was sleeping in the car. We were on a tight schedule because my son-in-law, a doctor, had to begin a shift at the hospital the next day and we cutting it pretty closely to get home in time.

"I started the journey quite awake, as I had prepared before with adequate rest and lots of coffee. I had done this trip before, even during these early morning hours. Suddenly, drowsiness came over me, which meant that I was seconds away from falling asleep. I knew I had to pull over, but I didn't know where I was, as I had not anticipated stopping. I knew I had to do something and found myself in the deceleration lane at the edge of the traffic lanes. It allowed me to reduce my speed, but I still knew that I could fall asleep in a split second, which would've been incredibly dangerous. Off the highway, I found my car driving directly into a parking lot. I was amazed. We usually would have to drive a while before being able to pull into an AA lot. I looked at the clock it was 3:10 a.m. I decided I would sleep for one hour, and that would not take us off of our schedule. I was grateful to have found a safe space to stop.

"What happened next was so surreal. I transitioned from drowsiness to asleep. In those few minutes, Michael appeared to me in quite a panic, 'Is everything alright?' he asked me over and over again. He startled me, but seemed to be relieved that we had made it to the side of the road. I tried to hug him, but he wouldn't allow me to hold him.

'You must go back now. You must go.' He made me understand they were waiting for me. I didn't want to leave him.

"Suddenly from the back, my son-in-law, Vinny, jolts awake, 'What just happened! Where are we?' he cried. The clock said 3:20. Where had I been those 10 minutes?

"I do know that Michael was with me, like an angel, and he guided me gently back to safety."

FDNY Remembers 12 Who Succumbed to 9/11-related Illnesses
Published: September 06, 2013
Reprinted with Permission from FDNY

During the dedication ceremony, family members placed roses at the memorial when their loved ones' name was read.

The FDNY remembered and honored the memory of 12 members who died due to 9/11-related illnesses in the last year, adding their names to a memorial plaque at FDNY Headquarters on Sept. 6th.

The added names included: Deputy Assistant Chief of EMS John McFarland, EMS Operations; Battalion Chief John Corcoran, Battalion 52; Lieutenant Marty Fullam, Ladder 87; Lieutenant Patrick Sullivan, Ladder 58; **Firefighter Michael Behette, Ladder 172;** Firefighter Andrew Dal Cortivo, Engine 227; Firefighter Charles Jones, Ladder 165; Firefighter Michael Mongelli, Battalion 39; Firefighter Larry Sullivan, Rescue 5; Paramedic Ruben Berrios, Station 20; EMT Anthony Ficara, Station 43; and EMT Joseph Schiumo, Station 20.

"Each of these FDNY members answered the call on Sept. 11, 2001, and in the weeks that followed in a desperate search to bring home our fallen members," Fire Commissioner Salvatore Cassano said. "And now we watch as these brave men and women fight brave battles against disease. Unfortunately, these are fights that few people ever win."

The plaque lists the names of 64 additional men and women of the FDNY who have tragically died due to 9/11-related illnesses.

"We are proud of what each of them did at the World Trade Center," Chief of Department Edward Kilduff said. "We appreciate their contribution and their sacrifice."

Hundreds of FDNY members attended the ceremony, standing beside the families of those lost.

"This ceremony is a tradition in the Department," Firefighter Joseph Esposito from Rescue 5 said. "We want the families to understand that we will never forget."

Street Naming Ceremony

In October of 2012, less than one month after Michael's passing, it was evident that something needed to be done to honor Michael's memory in the Brooklyn streets where he was raised.

Representative Michael Grimm and State Senator Marty Golden sent a letter to Community Board 10 Chairwoman Joanne Seminara in support of naming the northeast corner of 5 th Avenue and 85th Street "Firefighter Michael G. Behette 9/11 Memorial Way." At the family's request, Rep. Grimm and Senator Golden were ready to lend their full support. They believed that Michael was a selfless family and community member, a faithful public servant, and an American hero.

By October 18th, The Bay Ridge Eagle reported that the proposal was put on the fast track. Community Board 10 had recently adopted new rules regarding street naming requests, including a provision re-quiring a two-year waiting period before a street could be named for an individual.

However, Board 10 Chairman Joanne Seminara told members at their October 15 th meeting that an exception will be made for Behette. "After consulting with the executive committee this week, I have decided to make a decision in connection with the application in honor of Michael Behette, a firefighter who we understand died as a result of injuries he sustained Sept. 11, 2001, given that his un-timely death relates back to the tragic day more than 10 years ago, when so many other heroes, heroines, and innocent victims were lost," she said.

"Firefighter Michael Behette was an example to us all. His dedication to the recovery efforts is a reminder of the service and sacrifice of our bravest to help move our city forward after we were attacked," Golden said.

Letter to Chairwoman Joanne Seminara:

October 3, 2012
Dear Chairwoman Seminara,
We are writing in support of the proposed name for public area, "Firefighter Michael G. Behette 9/11 Memorial Way," for the northeast corner of 5th Avenue and 85th Street, submitted by Madeleine Behette. Michael Behette was a selfless family and community member, a faithful public servant, and an American hero.

Under the proposal, Michael Behette's name will continue to serve this community as a tribute to all those who have sacrificed their lives in service to our City and Nation, and as a reminder of our common values. We understand that the guidelines for naming public areas specify that the honoree must be deceased for not less than two years at the time of application submission. However, because Mr. Behette died as a result of such heroic acts and exceptional circumstances, we are asking the Board to waive this requirement. We believe Mr. Behette's legacy of courage, humility, and service deserves to be honored, and that we must pursue every opportunity for such stories to be acknowledged, lest we or our children ever forget.

We wish to express our strong interest in a favorable determination for Ms. Behette as she seeks recognition for her son. Thank you for your time and attention in this matter; your consideration is greatly appreciated. We look forward to the Board's decision.
Sincerely,
Michael G. Grimm, Member of Congress
Marty Golden, State Senator

On April 15, 2013
The Traffic and Transportation Committee approved the following Motion.

Motion: CB10 to approve the street-naming request for Firefighter Michael G. Behette 9/11 Memorial Way, northeast corner of 85th Street.

On May 17, 2014, a day that began much like September 11, 2001, clear skies and sunshine, the corner of 85th Street and 5th Avenue in Brooklyn, NY was co-named *"Firefighter Michael G. Behette 9/11 Memorial Way."*

Hundreds of people gathered in the streets and sat in the assembly structured by the 68th Precinct and the staff of Councilman Vincent Gentile's office, spearheaded by Sara Steinweiss, Councilman Gentile's event planner.

The ceremony, beginning with the presentation of Colors and the national anthem sung beautifully by David Rodriquez, known as America's Tenor, also a former NYPD.

During his invocation, Father Antoine Risk discussed the feelings evoked by men, women, and children that visited the Vietnam War Memorial in Washington DC. He compared the slow approach people took towards the wall. He talked about how a calmness and slowness came over one as they stop to remember the name of a loved one or even an unknown soldier who had sacrificed his life during the Vietnam War. The wall lists 58,000 Americans who gave their lives in service to their country.

Like the wall that heals, the street signs we use to commemorate our heroes will serve as a reminder for those living in the moment and for generations to come.

It seemed appropriate that this day would occur a few days after the opening of the 9/11 Memorial Museum. The intricately-detailed museum with artifacts telling 9/11 victims' story in a somber setting is located at 180 Greenwich St, New York, NY 10007.

The memorial museum commemorates the lives of those who perished on September 11, 2001 and February 26, 1993 and provides visitors with the opportunity to learn about the men, women and children who died.

At the ceremony, remarks were made by Honorable Salvatore Cassano, New York City Commissioner, during his last week serving as Fire Commissioner for the City of New York.

Senator Golden spoke of the pride he had having been friends with the Behette family for many years, and his own time as a New York City police officer much like Michael's mom, Madeleine, had been.

Honorable Nicole Malliotakis spoke about the importance of continuing to educate this and future generations about the history of the event through the museum and memorials that remind citizens of viable, dedicated men and women such as Mike Behette.

A beautiful rendition of the Beatles' *Let It Be* was sung by Vanessa Modafferi.

Firefighter and friend, John Diodato, reminded us that Michael was one of the most decorated men at their firehouse and that while off duty, he also responded to Crash 587 at the Rockaways, when an American Airlines jetliner bound from New York to Santo Domingo with 260 people aboard plunged into a neighborhood in Queens minutes after takeoff. No one on the plane survived.

As Council Member Vincent Gentile continued to host the event, others spoke of Michael's contribution to the community and society. Michael's family was also presented with a proclamation from the NYC Borough Advocate for Service and the Highest Achievement.

Also on the panel were FDNY Danny Price and Lynda Thomson, friends and colleagues of Mike. Danny Price is active in the FDNY Fire Family Transport Foundation, a non-profit organization that provides transportation services to firefighters and their families in their times of greatest need. A FDNY Family Transport Vehicle Truck, which was donated by the family, could be seen in the background proudly featuring a picture of Mike in this uniform. It was a similar van that was available to Michael's family during his illness and passing.

After a moving unveiling of the street sign with the Behette family and the FDNY Emerald Society Bags and Drums and a blessing of the sign by Msgr. David Cassato, Pastor at St. Athanasias, the friends, family, and community were invited to a luncheon, hosted by Madeleine Behette.

In early days of urban development, streets were typically named after landmarks such as Canal Street, or topographic features such as Water Street. Of course, location was also a common factor, as in East or Upper. Major streets were often given names of power such as State or King, and then there were or heroes and leaders, Washington, Martin Luther King, and Kennedy. In Brooklyn today, on the corner of 8th Street and 5th Avenue, a street once named in logical organized grids is renamed Firefighter Michael G. Behette 9/11 Memorial Way. It will honor the fallen firefighter who once grew up on the same block. It will be a lesson for students who go to school in the area as they hopefully learn about citizenship. Mike was a hero and paid the ultimate sacrifice for his dedicated citizenship. It's a great way to keep his memory alive, and this community will never forget the sacrifice that he and his family made.

Brooklyn Daily Eagle
  Brooklyn Street renamed in honor of fallen firefighter Michael Behette
By Paula Katinas

- *Source: Home Reporter News*
- *Published: 05/22/2014 01:48 AM (Reprinted with Permission)*

In the wake of 9/11, Brooklynite and firefighter Michael Behette cut his vacation in the Florida Keys short to be with his comrades at Ground Zero.

On September 17, 2012, Behette died at the age of 55. In recognition of his work and spirit, hundreds gathered at the corner of 85th Street and Fifth Avenue for the street renaming ceremony. The corner was renamed "Firefighter Michael G. Behette 9/11 Memorial Way." "I feel sort of an honor to my son for his legacy, his need to be remembered," said Madeleine Behette, his mother, at the memorial. She stayed strong as she remembered the times that her son would act as a peacemaker. Behette was states away when he heard about the World Trade Center. Naturally, he tried to find a flight home to New York City but, with no available trains and planes, he rented a car. Almost 1,500 miles away from home, he drove 24 hours straight, while being clocked for driving 90 miles per hour. When he finally got there, he joined others on the pile. After retiring in 2002, Behette spent the next several years with family. In 2011, he was diagnosed with lung cancer, directly related to the dust and exposure to the air from all those months working on the pile. Over 11 years later, he died. Following his parents' footsteps, Behette started out as a police officer. In 1981, he joined the Fire Department of New York and served his community for over 20 years at Ladder 172, Engine 330 in Bensonhurst.

Marianna Randazzo, a friend of Michael's for over 40 years, is composing a book about Michael, which will include a collection of stories from those who knew him. "He was the type of person who just made everyone feel important, he would give whoever he was with his undivided attention," she said.

"To put it simply, we named pieces of our city because of people who help keep us together, people like firefighter Michael Behette," said Councilmember Vincent Gentile at the dedication, and so it seems only right that we honor Michael and his enduring legacy by dedicating a part of the city he loved so much in his everlasting memory and what better place to commemorate Michael than right here, down the block from where he grew up and where his mother Madeleine still lives today."

At the naming ceremony, the streets were closed off, Firefighter officials including Commissioner Salvatore Cassano, local politicians, the fire rescue truck that was donated to the department in Michael's name and hundreds of friends, family and local citizens joined in for the naming service.

(Top Left) Fire Family Transport Vehicle donated by the Behette family and Engine 330, Ladder 172. (Top Right) Sign being unveiled (Middle): Street naming ceremony, 85ᵗʰ Street and 5ᵗʰ Avenue, Firefighter Michael G. Behette, 9/11 Memorial Way. (Bottom) Behette family and city officials holding street sign

BROOKLYN MEDIA GROUP • MAY 22 - MAY 28, 2014

Firefighter Michael G. Behette
9/11 Memorial Way

BROOKLYN MEDIA GROUP/Photo by James Coppola
Family, friends and elected officials posed with the sign memorializing late Firefighter Michael Behette.

Memorializing Michael Behette

A Letter and Prayer to my Son

Dear Michael,

Michael, I love you, mama. I love you so much and I need your million-dollar hugs.

I prayed and prayed for a miracle, and all of your friends and your sister, Marguerite, and your brother, Tony, and their families prayed for you, too.

Michael, you are a very kind, a very caring, helpful, loving, selfless, compassionate, and kind-hearted person. You, Michael, have a pure heart and remember what Jesus said: "Blessed are the pure of heart for they shall see God." Thank you, dear Jesus, for giving me my son Michael, a pure heart.

Michael, I am sure you are in heaven with Jesus now, and I ask St. Joseph while Jesus sleeps in his arms to press him in your name and kiss his fine head for you and to ask Jesus to return the kiss to you. Michael, when you drew your dying breath and I prayed for you, Michael, the devotion to the Drops of Blood lost by our Lord Jesus Christ on his way to Calvary at your intention and Jesus will concede to you the following five graces:

1. *The plenary indulgence and remittance of your sins. Michael, your sins are forgiven.*
2. *Michael, you will be free from the pain of Purgatory.*
3. *Michael, if you should die before completing the said three years, for you it will be the same as if I had completed them for you. I will continue praying them.*

4. *Michael, it will be upon your death the same as if you had shed all your blood for the holy faith. Jesus will descend from heaven the same as if you had shed all your blood for the holy faith.*
5. *Jesus descended from heaven to take your soul and that of your relatives until the fourth generation.*

Michael, please don't get mad at me for crying. I know you told me I break your heart seeing me cry. I miss you so much, and I am asking our Lord Jesus Christ and Mama Mary to help me cope with this loss of not seeing you anymore, and I cannot wait until the day I will be re-united with my son, Michael, my moonshine.

You were my strength, my joy, my love, my caregiver, my everything. You worried too much about me, your mama.

You were a pure hearted son who went out of his way to make friends and family and me, your mama, happy. Michael, we are all going to miss your funny stories. You brought so much happiness to my life in your 55 years on earth.

I promise you that when I am finished my work here, I will ask the Lord to purify my spirit and ask the Lord to unite me with you.

Our heavenly Father knows that you risked your own life when you heard about the attacks on the Trade Center. You abandoned your cruise and all of your belongings and you sped home back to NYC to help out. You even got a speeding ticket and went straight to Ground Zero to help your comrades and all who needed help. Your pain and suffering began in early 2011 and lasted until September 17, 2012.

- *Jesus endured His pain and suffering and was nailed and died on the cross for our salvation.*
- *You joined His suffering and His work of redemption, as you suffered and was crucified on that bed on which you died.*
- *Jesus fasted for 40 days and 40 nights. Michael, because of your declining health, Calvary refused you food and water from August 1, 2012 to September 17, 2012.*

- *Jesus loved his mother and ensured that His Mother was taken care of while she was on earth, and she in turn loved Him so much, she accepted the help provided to fulfill His wishes to be the Mother of all.*
- *You, Michael, loved me so much you ensured that I am well taken care of through friends and family, and in turn I love you so much that I accepted the help you're providing and to fulfill your wishes to help all those who need me.*
- *Like Christ, you were thirsty and requested some water. No water was given, yet like Christ, a small sponge was soaked and placed on your lips to lubricate them.*
- *Michael, in my heart I feel that you are a saint. I will be talking with you every day of my life, and I will ask for your prayers from heavers for you, along with Christ, have become our intercessor.*
- *Michael, now that you are in the Divine World, you can see my heart and mind and know that I did the best I knew how, just as your father, George, did, yet we failed many times. For those times, my pure-hearted son, we ask you to forgive us.*
- *Michael, I trust and believe that you are in a better place where there is neither pain, nor sorrow or tears. Your deep desire is to help so many people at the same time, yet while on earth you were restricted from doing so. You are now free from restrictions and you are free to do all that you want to do and be simultaneously in as many places as you desire. You began your work on earth by helping thousands of people in different ways. Now begins your work to help millions who continue to need you.*

Rest in peace, my pure-hearted son. Ask our loving Lord to give us the gift of His peace that surpasses all human understanding and the grace to accept it. As we confess in our Creed, we believe in the communion of saints. I believe and trust that we will always be united in Christ.
Love you,
Your Mama

Afterward

This book was written with the intention of offering some solace to the Behette family and friends. As each day passes and life moves forward, I learn more about the beautiful, kind, fun-loving man that was known by many monikers. He was a truly fine person who lived life with the passion of a man who seemed to know his time on earth would be too short to live by somebody else's dreams, so he fulfilled his own. He was also a man who believed in sharing the good times with friends, girlfriends and family members, old and new. Michael possessed affection for life and for those he loved, and he had a true dynamism that comes along so rarely. If you were a friend of Michael's, in most circumstances you were a friend for life.

In compiling the stories for this book, I have found that if there is one truth in this world, it is that people will never have an undesirable word to say about Michael Behette. I hope that in these pages I have done him justice.

Thank you,

Marianna Randazzo